All English-language scripture quotations, unless otherwise noted, are taken from the King James Version of the 1611 A.D. Holy Bible [KJV].

All Amharic-language scripture quotations, unless otherwise noted, are taken the *Emperor's Bible*, the 1961/2 A.D. Authorized H.I.M. HAILE SELLASSIE I Revised Amharic Bible [RAB].

Published by the Lion of Judah Society, *www.lojsociety.org*

Our mission is to bring good tidings, that publisheth peace; that bringeth good tidings of good, that saith to Zion, Thy God reigneth. – Isaiah 52:7

Printed in the United States of America.

THE LION OF JUDAH SOCIETY OF
HIS IMPERIAL MAJESTY (LOJS)
PUBLISHED BY: H.H. RAS IADONIS TAFARI,
& H.H. WOIZERO TEHETENA GIRMA-ASFAW
OF THE LION OF JUDAH SOCIETY (LOJS)
IMPERIAL PUBLISHERS TO THE H.I.M. UNIVERSITIES, COLLEGES &
CHRISTIAN [TEWAHEDO] CHURCHES

©1991-2011 LOJ SOCIETY-TM

TECHNOLOGIES. MINISTRIES.

የዮሐንስ ወንጌል 1፥14

ቃልም ሥጋ ሆነ፤ ጸጋንና እውነትንም ተመልቶ በእኛ አደረ፤ አንድ ልጅም ከአባቱ ዘንድ እንዳለው ክብር የሆነው ክብሩን አየን።

እኔ አባት እሆነዋለሁ እርሱም ልጅ ይሆነኛል

— ወደ ዕብራውያን 1:5

"The AMHARA race must know that it has an
obligation on its part to work in the technical field, no
matter at what level. To preserve the heritage of
one's honour and culture is praiseworthy,
but to exceed the limits may prove detrimental."
– **H.I.M. HAILE SELLASSIE I**

ሞዓ ፡ አንበሳ ፡ ዘእምነገደ ፡ ይሁዳ ።

ቀዳማዊ ፡ ኃይለ ፡ ሥላሴ ።

ሥዩመ ፡ እግዚአብሔር ፡ ንጉሠ ፡ ነገሥት ፡ ዘኢትዮጵያ ።

AMHARIC COMPUTER GLOSSARY

A-Z

TABLE OF CONTENTS

Ethiopic Fidel Charts, aka *Syllabaries*   page 13

Foreword by compiler, Ras Iadonis Tafari`
    page 19

Picture of Dr. Aberra Molla & H.I.M.   page 21

Introduction to the 1ˢᵗ Edition   **page 23**

African Unity & Telecommunications   **page 27**

H.I.M. Haile Selassie I Global View   page 29

Amharic Computer Glossary – A   page 33

Amharic Computer Glossary – B   page 63

Amharic Computer Glossary – C   page 72

Amharic Computer Glossary – D   page 92

Amharic Computer Glossary – E   page 108

Amharic Computer Glossary – F   page 116

Amharic Computer Glossary – G   page 120

Amharic Computer Glossary – H   page 122

Amharic Computer Glossary – I   page 129

Amharic Computer Glossary – J   page 132

Amharic Computer Glossary – K   page 134

Amharic Computer Glossary – L   page 136

Amharic Computer Glossary – M   page 140

Amharic Computer Glossary – N   page 149

Amharic Computer Glossary – O   page 151

Amharic Computer Glossary – P   page 153

Amharic Computer Glossary – Q   page 164

Amharic Computer Glossary – R   page 166

Amharic Computer Glossary – S   page 177

Amharic Computer Glossary – T   page 187

Amharic Computer Glossary – U   page 193

Amharic Computer Glossary – V   page 197

Amharic Computer Glossary – W   page 199

Amharic Computer Glossary – X   page 201

Amharic Computer Glossary – Y   page 202

Amharic Computer Glossary – Z   page 203

Appendix A & B: **page 205**

Appendix A (origins of *Bits*)   page 209

Appendix B (origins of *Bytes*)   page 219

The Ethiopic (Ge'ez-based) Fidel, also called: The Amharic Syllabary

ሀ	ሁ	ሂ	ሃ	ሄ	ህ	ሆ	ወ	ዉ	ዊ	ዋ	ዌ	ው	ዎ	
ለ	ሉ	ሊ	ላ	ሌ	ል	ሎ	ዐ	ዑ	ዒ	ዓ	ዔ	ዕ	ዖ	
ሐ	ሑ	ሒ	ሓ	ሔ	ሕ	ሖ	ዘ	ዙ	ዚ	ዛ	ዜ	ዝ	ዞ	
መ	ሙ	ሚ	ማ	ሜ	ም	ሞ	ዠ	ዡ	ዢ	ዣ	ዤ	ዥ	ዦ	
ሠ	ሡ	ሢ	ሣ	ሤ	ሥ	ሦ	የ	ዩ	ዪ	ያ	ዬ	ይ	ዮ	
ረ	ሩ	ሪ	ራ	ሬ	ር	ሮ	ደ	ዱ	ዲ	ዳ	ዴ	ድ	ዶ	
ሰ	ሱ	ሲ	ሳ	ሴ	ስ	ሶ	ጀ	ጁ	ጂ	ጃ	ጄ	ጅ	ጆ	
ሸ	ሹ	ሺ	ሻ	ሼ	ሽ	ሾ	ገ	ጉ	ጊ	ጋ	ጌ	ግ	ጎ	
ቀ	ቁ	ቂ	ቃ	ቄ	ቅ	ቆ	ጠ	ጡ	ጢ	ጣ	ጤ	ጥ	ጦ	
በ	ቡ	ቢ	ባ	ቤ	ብ	ቦ	ጨ	ጩ	ጪ	ጫ	ጬ	ጭ	ጮ	
ተ	ቱ	ቲ	ታ	ቴ	ት	ቶ	ጸ	ጹ	ጺ	ጻ	ጼ	ጽ	ጾ	
ቸ	ቹ	ቺ	ቻ	ቼ	ች	ቾ	ፀ	ፁ	ፂ	ፃ	ፄ	ፅ	ፆ	
ኀ	ኁ	ኂ	ኃ	ኄ	ኅ	ኆ	ፈ	ፉ	ፊ	ፋ	ፌ	ፍ	ፎ	
ነ	ኑ	ኒ	ና	ኔ	ን	ኖ	ፐ	ፑ	ፒ	ፓ	ፔ	ፕ	ፖ	
ኘ	ኙ	ኚ	ኛ	ኜ	ኝ	ኞ								
አ	ኡ	ኢ	ኣ	ኤ	እ	ኦ								
ከ	ኩ	ኪ	ካ	ኬ	ክ	ኮ								
ኸ	ኹ	ኺ	ኻ	ኼ	ኽ	ኾ								

ABCDEFGHIJKL
MNOPQRSTUVW
XYZ

ኰ	ኵ	ኲ	ኳ	ኴ		፩ ፪ ፫ ፬ ፭ ፮ ፯ ፰ ፱ ፲
ጐ	ጕ	ጒ	ጓ	ጔ		1 2 3 4 5 6 7 8 9 10
ቈ	ቊ	ቋ	ቌ	ቈ		፳ ፴ ፵ ፶ ፷ ፸
ኈ	ኍ	ኊ	ኋ	ኌ		20 30 40 50 60 70
						፹ ፺ ፻ ፼
						80 90 100 1000

ጪ ሟ ሯ ሷ ሿ ቧ ቷ ቿ ኗ ኟ ዟ ዧ ደ ጧ ጯ ጿ ፏ

	0	1	2	3	4	5	6	7	8	9	A	B	C	D	E	F
0x1200	ሀ	ሁ	ሂ	ሃ	ሄ	ህ	ሆ		ለ	ሉ	ሊ	ላ	ሌ	ል	ሎ	ሏ
0x1210	ሐ	ሑ	ሒ	ሓ	ሔ	ሕ	ሖ	ሗ	መ	ሙ	ሚ	ማ	ሜ	ም	ሞ	ሟ
0x1220	ሠ	ሡ	ሢ	ሣ	ሤ	ሥ	ሦ	ሧ	ረ	ሩ	ሪ	ራ	ሬ	ር	ሮ	ሯ
0x1230	ሰ	ሱ	ሲ	ሳ	ሴ	ስ	ሶ	ሷ	ሸ	ሹ	ሺ	ሻ	ሼ	ሽ	ሾ	ሿ
0x1240	ቀ	ቁ	ቂ	ቃ	ቄ	ቅ	ቆ		ቈ		ቊ	ቋ	ቌ	ቍ		
0x1250	ቐ	ቑ	ቒ	ቓ	ቔ	ቕ	ቖ		ቘ		ቚ	ቛ	ቜ	ቝ		
0x1260	በ	ቡ	ቢ	ባ	ቤ	ብ	ቦ	ቧ	ቨ	ቩ	ቪ	ቫ	ቬ	ቭ	ቮ	ቯ
0x1270	ተ	ቱ	ቲ	ታ	ቴ	ት	ቶ	ቷ	ቸ	ቹ	ቺ	ቻ	ቼ	ች	ቾ	ቿ
0x1280	ኀ	ኁ	ኂ	ኃ	ኄ	ኅ	ኆ		ኈ		ኊ	ኋ	ኌ	ኍ		
0x1290	ነ	ኑ	ኒ	ና	ኔ	ን	ኖ	ኗ	ኘ	ኙ	ኚ	ኛ	ኜ	ኝ	ኞ	ኟ
0x12A0	አ	ኡ	ኢ	ኣ	ኤ	እ	ኦ	ኧ	ከ	ኩ	ኪ	ካ	ኬ	ክ	ኮ	
0x12B0	ኰ		ኲ	ኳ	ኴ	ኵ			ኸ	ኹ	ኺ	ኻ	ኼ	ኽ	ኾ	
0x12C0	ዀ		ዂ	ዃ	ዄ	ዅ			ወ	ዉ	ዊ	ዋ	ዌ	ው	ዎ	
0x12D0	ዐ	ዑ	ዒ	ዓ	ዔ	ዕ	ዖ		ዘ	ዙ	ዚ	ዛ	ዜ	ዝ	ዞ	ዟ
0x12E0	ዠ	ዡ	ዢ	ዣ	ዤ	ዥ	ዦ	ዧ	የ	ዩ	ዪ	ያ	ዬ	ይ	ዮ	ዯ
0x12F0	ደ	ዱ	ዲ	ዳ	ዴ	ድ	ዶ	ዷ	ዸ	ዹ	ዺ	ዻ	ዼ	ዽ	ዾ	ዿ
0x1300	ጀ	ጁ	ጂ	ጃ	ጄ	ጅ	ጆ	ጇ	ገ	ጉ	ጊ	ጋ	ጌ	ግ	ጎ	ጏ
0x1310	ጐ		ጒ	ጓ	ጔ	ጕ			ጘ	ጙ	ጚ	ጛ	ጜ	ጝ	ጞ	ጟ
0x1320	ጠ	ጡ	ጢ	ጣ	ጤ	ጥ	ጦ	ጧ	ጨ	ጩ	ጪ	ጫ	ጬ	ጭ	ጮ	ጯ
0x1330	ጰ	ጱ	ጲ	ጳ	ጴ	ጵ	ጶ	ጷ	ጸ	ጹ	ጺ	ጻ	ጼ	ጽ	ጾ	ጿ
0x1340	ፀ	ፁ	ፂ	ፃ	ፄ	ፅ	ፆ		ፈ	ፉ	ፊ	ፋ	ፌ	ፍ	ፎ	ፏ
0x1350	ፐ	ፑ	ፒ	ፓ	ፔ	ፕ	ፖ	ፗ	ፘ	ፙ	ፚ					
0x1360		፡	።	፣	፤	፥	፦	፧	፨	፩	፪	፫	፬	፭	፮	፯
0x1370	፰	፱	፲	፳	፴	፵	፶	፷	፸	፹	፺	፻	፼			
0x1380	ᎀ	ᎁ	ᎂ	ᎃ	ᎄ	ᎅ	ᎆ		ᎈ	ᎉ	ᎊ	ᎋ	ᎌ			
0x1390	᎐	᎑	᎒	᎓	᎔	᎕	᎖		᎘	᎙	᎚	᎛	᎜			
0x13A0	Ꭰ	Ꭱ	Ꭲ	Ꭳ	Ꭴ	Ꭵ	Ꭶ		Ꭸ	Ꭹ	Ꭺ	Ꭻ	Ꭼ			
0x13B0	Ꮀ	Ꮁ	Ꮂ	Ꮃ	Ꮄ	Ꮅ	Ꮆ		Ꮈ	Ꮉ	Ꮊ	Ꮋ	Ꮌ			
0xFDF0	ﷰ	ﷱ	ﷲ	ﷳ	ﷴ	ﷵ	ﷶ	ﷷ	ﷸ	ﷹ	ﷺ	ﷻ	﷼		﷾	﷿

Phonetic value	Old north-Semitic	Sinai script (after Grimme)	Thamudic		Ṣafatene		Liḥyanite	Mino-Sabaean	Old Abyssinian	Ethiopic (Geʿez)
			Old	New	true Ṣafatene	Umm eǧ-Ǧimāl				
a										
b										
g										
d										
h										
w										
z										
ḫ										
ṭ										
j										
k										
l										
m										
n										
s										
ʿ										
; south-sem. f										
ś										
q										
r										
š										
t										

17

Phonetic value	Thamudic		Ṣafatene			Lithyanite	Mino-Sabaean	Old Abyssinian	Ethiopic (Ge'ez)
	Old	New	True Ṣafatene		Umm eg-Ǧimāl				
ṣ	ヨΛ	ΛΠC	ΠΛΛΛV٢	⟩—	ПѲѴⱵ	Π	ΠЛ	ስ
ḍ	ⴼ#╫	##Η	人Ƴ	Ⴟ	ΨΜ	ΗΗ		
ṭ	✳✳	ℰ◦—◦	ℰℰℰ	ℰ	Ɨ↑↑	ℰ		
ḫ	ΚΧ	⅄ᵮΧ	Χ Χ	✗	ʓⱵⱵ	Ⴟℰ	ℰ	ⳇ
ḏ	ⳆΗ	ⵚΗ⟡⟡	ΗΗ#	⊙	⥾ℰ	Β	Β	ዐ
ẓ			⋃ЛⱵЛ∏	∏		ℰℰ		
ṗ							ℰℰℰ	⨉
p							⟨	Τ
g (γ)	Ⴀℰᵐ	ℰℲℲ	ᑕᒥ⟩ℰ	ℰ	Ⱶⱱ	∏		

Ethiopic Computing[1], then & now....

---

[1] See *Amarigna & Tigrigna Qal Hieroglyphs for Beginners*, by Legesse Allyn for more on the rediscovered commerce-based correspondences and linguistic

FOREWORD

Firstly, we would like to extend out sincere gratitude and thanks to all those native and diasporic Ethiopians who have contributed to the advance and dissemination of Ethiopic Computing in the 20th and into the 21st century, the New Millennium. There are many, some whom we know not of, and others who we desire to make mention of in this brief forward to the present volume and first edition of *"Amharic Computer-Based Glossary."* The first native Ethiopian that we name and credit here, is Dr. Aberra Molla – the founder of www.Ethiopic.com, a prolific Ethiopianist, scholar, inventor, scientist, writer and author of several noteworthy articles on topics concerning Ethiopian Subjects, and in particular, Ethiopic Computing. He was a graduate of H.I.M. Haile Selassie I University, now Addis Abeba University, and may be credited with being one of the initial, if not the first, to develop Ethiopic computing technology and software for a variety of applications. There is, however, some dispute amongst several Ethiopic developers and programmers of who deserves the primary accolades, or who was first. In fact, in our opinion, they all have contributed mightily, not without due and necessary competition of achieving the desired results, to the digitalization of the Ethiopic languages, particularly the Amharic, the official language of the Ethiopian Empire and present nation-state.

---

comparisons between root words, symbols, meanings and advanced technologies [or, Wisdom] of Ancient Ethiopia and Ancient *Kamite* Egypt.

Thus, we begin these commendations and expressions of gratitude, as above, with Dr. Molla and also find it appropriate to include the following names: Fesseha Atlaw, Yitna Firdyiwek, Daniel Admassie, Yonas Fisseha, Efrem Habteselassie, Fikre Yibrehu – to these, and other noteworthy Ethiopian developers and computer programmers, especially they who we are unable at the present writing to name or mention, have all, in their part, and many still continue to keep the *Lisane Negus*: Amharic and Ethiopic Computerization overall very much progressively active and alive in the present time, and well moving forwards ever onwards toward the future, that is, our New Ethiopian Age.

H.H. Ras Iadonis Tafari

POSTSCRIPT: Several Ethiopic-based computer sciences books are currently in compilation that will expand on the latest technologies, research and development in the varied fields of modern Ethiopic Computation featuring additional data and details that could not, due to space, be included in this brief desktop reference manual.

H.I.M. HAILE SELASSIE I – IMPERIAL ETHIOPIA'S 1ST PATRON OF TECHNOLOGY, EDUCATION & FINE ARTS...

Ethiopic Computing inventor, Dr. Aberra Molla gives a presentation to His Imperial Majesty, HAILE SELLASSIE I along with a group of officials, students and visitors.

INTRODUCTION

The Amharic Computer-Based Glossary presented in these pages is a compilation from various anonymous sources[2], on and offline. Due accreditation, however, must be given to the current technologically savvy generation of young and old Amharic-speaking Ethiopians, male and females, who have diligently sought to master the modern society and digital multimedia through "Ethiopian spectacles," and not be left behind in a rapidly changing and evolving age of globalization. Therefore, we generously thank all those Ethiopians, at home and abroad, those professionals and non-professionals alike, who have continuously contributed ideas, words, expressions, phrases and advanced technological terms towards the aggregation of the contents of this Glossary.

Thus, the said Glossary is by no means complete, rather a work-in-progress, especially in the sense that new digital developments, media, ideas, terms and words are continuously being modified, coined and circulated, even as we write now this Introduction to the present edition. However, it is sincerely hoped and indeed expected that the Ethiopic [GE'EZ] and Amharic keywords contained here will serve as a basis and foundation to build further upon, even while realizing the significant and ever-increasing

---

[2] With the exception of a Fantaw and an individual *fidelized* as ተፈራ—*Teffera*, we are not able sadly, at the present time, to accredit duly the possible Amharic coining, adaptations or even the first Ethiopic usages of the modern computer-based language and terminologies that we have compiled here in this volume.

impact that modern telecommunications is having upon our motherland Africa, Africans in the diaspora and at-home, not to mention the world-at-large. As language is said to be the key of communications between man and man, it is necessary and vital that clear, concise and precise words, terms, and phrases are learnt, understood and utilized by the modern generation of Ethiopians at home and abroad. This then, we may say, is the main intention of the publication of this edition of our proposed *Amharic Computer-Based Glossary*, published by the Lion of Judah Society of His Imperial Majesty (*www.lojsociety.org*).

Additional terms and references, along with a appropriate transcriptions, will be compiled further and presented in other volumes, either as a revision to this edition, or as entirely new subjects given more refined and selective treatment, discussion and presentation – all as the Lord wills, so will we, and those faithfully following our efforts here, do and even excel above and beyond that which we are attempting at present.

The great summit destined for us by our God and Father, the Great Creator, is not yet attained by the Sons of Ethiopia, nor will it be if we hesitate to courageously print, publish and "to disseminate the ancient Ethiopian culture" amongst the members of the Ethiopic corporate Body of Christ in His kingly character, at home and abroad. In this, our endeavour 'to secure Justice and maintain the integrity of Ethiopia, which is our divine heritage,' we must remember the wonderful counsel of H.I.M.

HAILE SELASSIE I, namely that – *"Education is the key."* And, to this we heartily agree and prayerfully say, "Amen, so be it."

H.H. Ras Iadonis Tafari
Wzo. Tehetena Girma-Asfaw

June 2011
LION OF JUDAH SOCIETY,
County of Kings, New York

AFRICAN UNITY AND TELECOMMUNICATIONS, Mar. 08, 1966

... The expansion and improvement of the intra-African telecommunications network is one of the basic necessities to attain Our goal of African unity. If we consider the present state of African telecommunications, we note that when any African country communicate with another African country by telephone or telegram it must often be made through transit centres situated outside Africa. These circuits are consequently expensive and often technically unusable and certainly not rapid. If this situation is not rectified in the near future the development of Africa in all fields will be seriously handicapped.

Rapid communication between African countries is one of the most important tools by which We can promote development in Africa. It is to be remembered that we have discussed this problem several times, but the anticipated progress of intra-African communications has not been achieved.

It is believed that you are here today to discuss collectively the Dakar African Telecommunications Plan of Rome of 1963 and the methods by which the implementation of these plans can be achieved.

To fulfill these plans immediately on a continental basis would inevitably call for very heavy investment. It will thus probably be necessary to implement them step by step in accordance with Our economic capabilities.

We, therefore, hope that you will make a serious effort

to carry out your task and reach a successful solution and that this conference will mark a milestone in the development of African telecommunications....

H.I.M. HAILE SELASSIE, THE FIRST
March 08, 1966

H.I.M. HAILE SELLASSIE I, *Our Abba,*
The Father of Progressive Africa

EMPEROR HAILE SELASSIE I
WORLD TOUR

a.k.a. ETHIOPIA ON THE MARCH

Amharic Computer Glossary
Glossary
A-Z

Amharic Computer Glossary – A

- 1 32-bit
- 2 3D
- 3 abandon
- 4 abort
- 5 About
- 6 Absolute path
- 7 absolute reference
- 8 absolute value
- 9 accelerator key
- 10 accent
- 11 accent acute
- 12 Accent Breve
- 13 accent circumflex
- 14 Accent Dieresis
- 15 accent grave
- 16 Accent Macron
- 17 Accent Tilde
- 18 Accept
- 19 access
- 20 access code
- 21 access key
- 22 access permission

- 23 access time
- 24 Accessibility
- 25 accessory
- 26 account
  - o 26.1 user account
- 27 account number
- 28 across
- 29 action
- 30 activate
- 31 actual
- 32 adapter
- 33 add-on
- 34 adhoc (wireless network)
- 35 advance
- 36 advanced
- 37 after
- 38 again
- 39 align
- 40 always
- 41 amount
- 42 analyze
- 43 angle
- 44 answer
- 45 any

- 46 Aperture Value
- 47 appear
- 48 architecture
- 49 around
- 50 arrange
- 51 assistant
- 52 at least
- 53 at most
- 54 attach
- 55 attack
- 56 ASCII
- 57 auto Arrange
- 58 auto filter
- 59 auto fit
- 60 axe
- 61 abort
- 62 about
- 63 absolute
- 64 accelerator
- 65 accent
- 66 accept
- 67 access (n)
- 68 access (v)
- 69 permission

- 70 accessibility
- 71 accessing
- 72 accessories
- 73 account
- 74 accuracy
- 75 accurate
- 76 acronym
- 77 action
- 78 actions menu
- 79 activate
- 80 active
- 81 acute
- 82 adapter
- 83 add
- 84 add-on help
- 85 add-on
- 86 address book
- 87 address
- 88 adjust
- 89 administrator setup
- 90 administrator
- 91 affect
- 92 alert (n)
- 93 alert (v)

- 94 alert me
- 95 algorithm
- 96 alias
- 97 alignment
- 98 all
- 99 allocate
- 100 allocation (n)
- 101 allocation (v)
- 102 allow popup from this site
- 103 allow
- 104 alphabetic text character
- 105 alphabetic
- 106 alter
- 107 alternative
- 108 ampersand
- 109 anchor
- 110 angle brackets
- 111 animate
- 112 animation
- 113 anniversary
- 114 anonymity
- 115 anonymous
- 116 antivirus
- 117 apostrophe

- 118 apparition
- 119 appears to be
- 120 applet
- 121 application (s)
- 122 application
- 123 apply
- 124 appointment
- 125 arc
- 126 arccosine
- 127 archive (n)
- 128 archive (v)
- 129 archiving
- 130 argument
- 131 array formula
- 132 array
- 133 arrow
- 134 article
- 135 artificial
- 136 ascending
- 137 assign
- 138 assigned
- 139 associate
- 140 association
- 141 asterisk

- 142 at
- 143 attachment
- 144 attention
- 145 attribute(s)
- 146 atttach
- 147 audio
- 148 authenticate
- 149 authentication
- 150 authenticity
- 151 author
- 152 authorization
- 153 auto correct
- 154 auto detected
- 155 auto
- 156 auto-detect
- 157 auto-reliable
- 158 autoFormat (n)
- 159 autoFormat (v)
- 160 autocomplete
- 161 autoformat
- 162 autoload
- 163 automatic detection
- 164 automatic
- 165 updating

- 166 available
- 167 average
- 168 axis

32-bit

1. 32-ቢት

3D

1. በለ3 አቅጣጫ
2. ስሉስገጽ
3. 3-ል (ል- ልኬት)
4. 3-ስ (ስ-ስፍረት)

abandon

1. ተው
2. መተው

abort

1. አጨንግፍ
2. ማጨንገፍ

About

1. ስለ

Absolute path

1. ፍቱም ፈለግ

2. ፍቱም ዱካ

absolute reference

ፍፀም ማጣቀሻ

absolute value

1. ፍፀም እሴት

2. ገጥረ እሴት

accelerator key

1. አፍጣኝ ቁልፍ

accent

1. ትእምርት

accent acute

1. ሹል ትእምርት

2. ሹል አመልካች

3. ስል ትእምርት

Accent Breve

1. ቄንፅል ትዕምርት

accent circumflex

1. ዝባላ ትእምርት
2. ዝባላ አመልካች (ዝባላ-ዝቅዝቅ ባላ)

Accent Dieresis

1. ትዕምርተ ጥቅስ

accent grave

1. ክብድ ትእምርት

Accent Macron

1. ትዕምርተ ማክሮን

Accent Tilde

1. ትዕምርተ ቲልደ

Accept

1. መቀበል
2. ተቀበል

access

1. መግባት

2. መዳረሻ

3. ድርሶሽ

4. ስድረስ(ግ)

access code

1. መዳረሻ ኮድ

access key

1. መዳረሻ ቁልፍ

access permission

1. መዳረሻ ፈቃድ

access time

1. መዳረሻ ጊዜ

Accessibility

1. አቅላይ

2. ተመቻችቶነት

3. ድርሶሽነት

4. አድርሶት

accessory

1. አቅላይ

2. ተቀጥላ

account

1. መዝገብ

user account

1. የተጠቃሚ መዝገብ

account number

1. መዝገብ ቁጥር

across

1. ባሻገር

action

1. ርምጃ

activate

1. አስነሳ (deactivate=አቁም፣ አስተኛ)

2. አንቃ

actual

    1. ትክክለኛ-መጠን

adapter

    1. አዛማጅ, አጣማጅ

add-on

    1. ቅጣይ

adhoc (wireless network)

    1. ተጋሪ
(see managed)

advance

    1. ይቅደም

advanced

    1. በጥልቀት

after

    1. በኋላ

again

    1. እንደገና

align

1. ይሰለፍ፡

always

1. ሁልጊዜ

amount

1. መጠን

analyze

1. ይመርመር

2. ይተነተን [3]

angle

1. ማዕዘን

answer

1. መልስ

any

1. ማንኛውም

---

[3] Fantaw 17:46, 18 May 2006 (UTC)

Aperture Value

1. የክፍተት እሴት

appear

1. ይታይ

architecture

1. መዋቅር

around

1. ዙሪያ

arrange

1. ይስተካከል

assistant

1. ረዳት

at least

1. በትንሹ

2. ቢያንስ

4

---

4 Fantaw 17:43, 18 May 2006 (UTC) ተፈራ 23:42, 20 May 2006 (UTC)

at most

1. በትልቁ

attach

1. አባሪ-ይደረግ

2. አያይዝ [5]

attack

1. መድፈር

2. መደፈር

ASCII

1. አስኪ. (የአሜሪካ የመረጃ መለዋወጫ ደረጃ ኮድ)

auto Arrange

1. በራስ-ገዝ ይስተካከል

auto filter

1. በራስ-ገዝ ይጣራ

auto fit

1. በራስ-ገዝ ይመጠን

---

[5] Fantaw 17:35, 18 May 2006 (UTC) ተፈራ 23:43, 20 May 2006 (UTC)

axe

   1. መጥረቢያ

abort

   1. ይቁም

about

   1. ስለ

absolute

   1. ፍፁም

accelerator

   1. አፍጣኝ

accent

   1. ማስረገጥ

accept

   1. ይቀበል

access (n)

   1. መግባት

access (v)

    1. ይገባ

permission

    1. ፈቃድ

accessibility

    1. የመግባት ባህሪ

accessing

    1. እየገባ ነው

accessories

    1. አጋዥ ፕሮግራሞች

account

    1. መዝገብ

accuracy

    1. ትክክለኛነት

accurate

    1. ትክክል

acronym

   1. ምሳፃሬ-ቃል

action

   1. ተግባር

actions menu

   1. የትግባሮች ሜኑ

activate

   1. ይሃድ

active

   1. ሃደት-ላይ

   2. ገቢር(ስ)(ቅ?)(ቢ አይጠብቅም)

acute

   1. አጣዳፊ

adapter

   1. መጣኝ

add

   1. ይጨመር

add-on help

1. የተቀጣይ-ፕሮግራም መመሪያ

add-on

1. ተቀጣይ-ፕሮግራም

address book

1. የአድራሻ መዝገብ

address

1. አድራሻ

adjust

1. ይስተካከል

administrator setup

1. የአስተዳዳሪ ስየማ

administrator

1. አስተዳዳሪ

affect

1. ተፅዕኖ

alert (n)

   1. ማስጠንቀቂያ

alert (v)

   1. ያስጠነቅቅ

alert me

   1. አስጠንቅቀኝ

algorithm

   1. አልጎሪዝም

alias

   1. ምስለኔ

alignment

   1. ማስተካከል

all

   1. ሁሉም

allocate

   1. ይደልደል

allocation (n)

   1. አደላደል

allocation (v)

   1. ድልደላ

allow popup from this site

   1. ከዚህ ገፅ ለሚመጡ ዘላይ መስኮቶች ይፈቀድ

allow

   1. ይፈቀድ

alphabetic text character

   1. የፊደል ቅደም-ተከተል ጽሐፍ

alphabetic

   1. የፍደል ቅደም ተከተል

alter

   1. ይቀየር

alternative

   1. አማራጭ

ampersand

1. የላቲን እና(&) ምልክት

anchor

1. መልሕቅ

angle brackets

1. ማዕዘን ቅንፍ

animate

1. ተንቀሳቃሽ-ምስል-ይሰራ

animation

1. ተንቀሳቃሽ-ምስል-መስራት

anniversary

1. መታሰቢያ ቀን

anonymity

1. ስም-ላይጠራ

anonymous

1. ስም-አልባ

2. ስምየለሽ

3. ስም-ድብቅ

antivirus

1. ፀረ-ቫይረስ

apostrophe

1. ጭረት

apparition

1. እንግዳ-ነገር

appears to be

1. ይመስላል

applet

1. ንዑስ-ፕሮግራም

application (s)

1. መጠቀሚያ ፕሮግራም

application

1. መጠቀሚያ ፕሮግራም

apply

   1. ይጠቀም

appointment

   1. ቀጠሮ

arc

   1. አርክ

arccosine

   1. አርክ-ኮሳይን

archive (n)

   1. ግምጃ-ቤት

archive (v)

   1. ይኑር

archiving

   1. ማኖር

   2. ማስቀመጥ

argument

   1. ወሳኝ-ተለዋጭ

array formula

1. ድርድር ፎርሙላ

array

1. ድርድር

arrow

1. ቀስት

article

1. ቁሳቁስ

artificial

1. አስመሳይ

ascending

1. ወጪ

assign

1. ይመደብ

assigned

1. ተመድቢል

associate

    1. ይገዳኝ

association

    1. ማገዳኘት

asterisk

    1. ኮከብ-ነጥብ

at

    1. በ

attachment

    1. አባሪ

attention

    1. ትኩረት

attribute(s)

    1. ጠባየ-እንቀጽ

    2. ባህሪ

atttach

    1. አባሪ-ይሁን

audio

    1. ድምፅ

authenticate

    1. ያረጋግጥ

authentication

    1. ማረጋገጥ

authenticity

    1. የተረጋገጠ-መሆን

author

    1. ደራሲ

authorization

    1. መፍቀድ

auto correct

    1. በራስ ይስተካከል

    2. በራስ-ገዝ ይስተካከል

auto detected

    1. በራስ-ገዝ የተገኘ

   1. ራስ

   2. በራስ-ገዝ

auto-detect

   1. በራስ-ገዝ ይገኝ

auto-reliable

   1. በራስ-ገዝ ይታመን

autoFormat (n)

   1. በራስገዝ-ማዘጋጀት

autoFormat (v)

   1. በራስገዝ-ይዘጋጅ

autocomplete

   1. በራስገዝ-ይሞላ

autoformat

   1. በራስገዝ-ማዘጋጀት

autoload

   1. በራስገዝ-ይምጣ

automatic detection

1. በራስ-ገዝ ማግኘት

automatic

1. በራስ-ገዝ

updating

1. ማሻሻል

available

1. አለ

average

1. ማዕከላዊ

axis

1. እንዝርት

[6]*Compiler & Editor's Note*

---

[6] See also – ምድብ: የኮምፒዩተር መድብለ-ቃላት

Amharic Computer Glossary – B

- 1 BACKSPACE key
- 2 BBS (Bulletin Board Service)
- 3 before
- 4 bell
- 5 Bidi options
- 6 binder
- 7 black
- 8 book
- 9 Boolean operations
- 10 Boolean
- 11 break
- 12 bring
- 13 build
- 14 back button
- 15 back
- 16 backend
- 17 background color
- 18 background
- 19 backslash(e)s
- 20 backslash
- 21 backup
- 22 backward compatible

- 23 backward moderated
- 24 backward
- 25 bad address
- 26 bad
- 27 baseline
- 28 baud
- 29 beam
- 30 beamer
- 31 beep
- 32 beginner
- 33 below
- 34 beta
- 35 bevel
- 36 bidirectional language
- 37 binary (adj)
- 38 binary (n)
- 39 bit
- 40 bitmap
- 41 blackandwhite
- 42 blank space
- 43 blank
- 44 busy
- 45 button

BACKSPACE key

1. የወደኋላ-ማጥፊያ ቁልፍ

BBS (Bulletin Board Service)

1. መልዕክት መለዋወጫ አገልግሎት

before

1. ቀድሞ

bell

1. ደወል

Bidi options

1. የቢዲ ምርጫዎች

binder

1. አቃፊ

black

1. ጥቁር

book

1. መጽሐፍ

Boolean operations

1. የቡልያን ስሌት

Boolean

1. ቡልያን

break

1. ይሰበር

2. ሰበር

bring

1. ይምጣ

2. አምጣ

build

1. ይገነባ

2. ገነባ

back button

1. የወደኋላ ቁልፍ

back

1. ኋላ

2. ወደኋላ [7]

backend

1. ከጀርባ

background color

1. የመደብ ቀለም [8]

background

1. መደብ

backslash(e)s

1. ወደኋላ-ያዘመመ-መስመር

backslash

1. ኋላአዝማሚ

2. ወደኋላ-ያዘመመ-መስመር [9]

backup

1. መጠባበቂያ-ኮፒ

[7] --Fantaw 20:45, 27 May 2006 (UTC)

[8] --ተፈራ 09:16, 13 May 2006 (UTC)

[9] --ተፈራ 09:16, 13 May 2006 (UTC)

2. መጠባበቂያ [10]

backward compatible

1. ወደኋላ ተስማሚ

backward moderated

1. ወደኋላ የሚስተናበር

backward

1. ወደኋላ

bad address

1. የተበላሽ አድራሽ

bad

1. የተበላሽ

2. አጉል [11]

==bandwidth== የባንድ-ስፋት ==banner== መፈክር ==bar== ማስጨ

baseline

1. መሠረታዊ-መስመር

---

[10] Fantaw 20:46, 27 May 2006 (UTC)
[11] Fantaw 20:49, 27 May 2006 (UTC)

baud

   1. ባውድ

beam

   1. ይተላለፍ

beamer

   1. አስተላላፊ

beep

   1. ጺጽ

beginner

   1. ጀማሪ

below

   1. ከስር

beta

   1. ሙከራ

bevel

   1. ሰያፍ-ጠርዝ

bidirectional language

  1. ባለሁለት አቅጣጫ ቋንቋ

binary (adj)

  1. ጥንድ

binary (n)

  1. ጥንዶ

bit

  1. ቢት

bitmap

  1. የቢት-ምስል

blackandwhite

  1. ጥቁርና-ነጭ

blank space

  1. ባዶ ስፍራ

blank

  1. ባዶ

blind carbon copy (bcc) አድራሻ-አልባ-የመልዕክት-ኮፒ block (a command) ይዘጋበት block (n) መዝጊያ block device የመዝጊያ-ቁስ blocked የተዘጋ body አካል bold (adj) ደማቅ bold (v) ይድመቅ bold button የማድመቂያ ቁልፍ bookmark (v) እልባት bookmark link ማገዳኛው እልባት ይደረግለት bookmark (n) እልባት boot disk መነሻ-ዲስክ boot drive መነሻ-ዲስክ boot መነሻ border relief ወሰን መለያ border(s) ወሰን bottom ታች bounce ይውጣ bouncing block መዝጊያ boundary ወሰን box ሳጥን bps ቢ.በስ braces አቃፊ brackets ቅንፎች breakpoint ለውጥ-ነጥብ brightness ድምቀት browse (for file) ቃኝ browse ቃኝ browser ቃኝ bubble (n) አረፋ buffer

1. ክፍል

2. ቋት

bugs ተውሳክ builder ገንቢ built-in ውስጣዊ bullet points ባለምልክት ነጥቦች bullet ምልክት bulleted list ባለምልክት ዝርዝር business ሙያ

busy

1. በስራ ላይ

2. ተይዟል

button

1. ቁልፍ

2. አዝራር

buttons: exit ቁልፎች፦ መውጫ byte(s) ባይት(ቶች)

Amharic Computer Glossary – C

- 1 computer
- 2 credential
- 3 crop
- 4 CAPS LOCK key
- 5 CD/CD-ROM/compact disk
- 6 CPU (central processing unit)
- 7 CRC
- 8 calendar
- 9 catalog
- 10 categories
- 11 center
- 12 channel
- 13 character
- 14 chat
- 15 check
- 16 checksum
- 17 classify
- 18 client
- 19 Clipboard

- 20 comparison
- 21 confirm
- 22 contact
- 23 continuous
- 24 corner
- 25 Ctrl (control)
- 26 currency
- 27 current
- 28 cache
- 29 calculator
- 30 call preference
- 31 waiting
- 32 call
- 33 call-in
- 34 call-out
- 35 callback
- 36 cancel
- 37 capital letters
- 38 capitalization
- 39 capitals
- 40 caps
- 41 caption
- 42 capture (v)
- 43 carbon copy (cc)

- 44 carriage return
- 45 carrying case
- 46 cascade
- 47 case sensitive
- 48 category
- 49 cell
- 50 certificate manager
- 51 certificate viewer
- 52 certificate
- 53 change
- 54 channel (n)
- 55 chapter
- 56 character set
- 57 chart
- 58 chat group
- 59 chat
- 60 check (n)
- 61 check (v)
- 62 check box
- 63 check for
- 64 checksum
- 65 child (hierarchy)
- 66 children (hierarchy)
- 67 chime

- 68 chip
- 69 choose
- 70 chooser
- 71 configuration file
- 72 configuration utility
- 73 configuration
- 74 configure
- 75 confirmation
- 76 conflict
- 77 connect to a server
- 78 connect
- 79 connection failure
- 80 connection string
- 81 connection
- 82 connector
- 83 constant
- 84 console
- 85 content
- 86 context
- 87 continue
- 88 contrast
- 89 control (n)
- 90 control (v)
- 91 critical

- 92 crop
- 93 cross

computer

1. አስሊ.

2. ቀማሪ

3. ኮምፑተር

credential

ማንነትመረጃ

crop

1. መመጠን

CAPS LOCK key

1. የላቲን-ትልቅ-ፊደሎች-ማስነሻ-ቁልፍ

CD/CD-ROM/compact disk

1. ሲዲ

CPU (central processing unit)

1. ማዕከላዊ አስሊ.

CRC

   1. ያልተጠበቀ ስህተት መቆጣጠሪያ

calendar

   1. ቀን መቁጠሪያ

catalog

   1. ማውጫ

categories

   1. ምድቦች

center

   1. ማዕከል

channel

character

   1. ፊደል

chat

   1. ተጫወት

   2. ውይይት

check

   1. መፈተሽ

   2. ፈትግ

checksum

   1. ቆጣሪ

   2. ቼክሰም

classify

   1. መድብ

client

   1. ጣሪ (server=ተጣሪ)

   2. ደንበኛ

Clipboard

   1. የቅጂ-ሰሌዳ

comparison

   1. ማመዛዘን

confirm

   1. ይስማሚል

2. ተስማማ

contact

1. ወዳጅ

continuous

1. የተያያዘ

corner

1. ጠርዝ

Ctrl (control)

1. የኮንትሮል መጥሪያ

currency

1. ገንዘብ

current

1. ወቅታዊ

cache

1. ካሽ

calculator

1. አስሊ

call preference

1. የመደወል ምርጫዎች

waiting

1. በመጠበቅ-ላይ

call

1. ጥሪ

call-in

1. ጥሪ..ከ

call-out

1. ጥሪ..ወደ

callback

1. ይደውሉልኝ-ጥሪ

cancel

1. ይቅር

2. ሰርዝ

capital letters

   1. ትልቅ-የላቲን-ፊደላት

capitalization

   1. ወደ ትልቅ-የላቲን-ፊደላት መቀየር

capitals

   1. ትልቅ-የላቲን-ፊደላት

caps

   1. ትልቅ የላቲን ፊደላት

caption

   1. ጥቅስ

capture (v)

   1. ይያዝ

   2. ያዝ

carbon copy (cc)

   1. ካርቦን ኮፒ (ካኮ)

   2. ግልባጭ

   3. ፎቶ ኮፒ

carriage return

1. መላሽ መጥሪያ

carrying case

1. መያዣ-ቦርሳ

cascade

1. እጅብ-ሂደት

case sensitive

1. ትልቅና ትንሽ የእንግሊዘኛ ፊደሎች የተለያየ አሴት አላቸው

category

1. ምድብ

cell

1. ክፍል

2. ህዋስ

3. አያድ

certificate manager

1. ምስክር አስተዳዳሪ

certificate viewer

    1. ምስክር-ቃል መመልከቻ

certificate

    1. ምስክር-ቃል

change

    1. ይለወጥ

channel (n)

    1. መስመር

chapter

    1. ምዕራፍ

character set

    1. የፊደል-ስብስብ

chart

    1. ስንጠረዥ

chat group

    1. የውይይት ክበብ

chat

    1. ውይይት

check (n)

    1. ማረጋገጥ

check (v)

    1. ይረጋገጥ

check box

    1. ማረጋገጫ-ሳጥን

check for

    1. ይረጋገጥ

checksum

    1. መቆጣጠሪያ-ድምር

child (hierarchy)

    1. ልጅ (ተወራራሽ)

children (hierarchy)

    1. ልጆች (ተወራራሽ)

chime

   1. ደወል

chip

   1. ኤሌክትሮ-ገል

choose

   1. ይመረጥ

chooser

   1. መራጭ

==chunks== ጕብጥ-ይዘት ==cipher== የሚስጢር-ኮድ ==ciphers== የሚስጢር-ኮዶች ==circle== ክብ ==citation== ሽልማት ==clash== ግጭት ==class== መደብ ==clear (a)== ይጽዳ ==clear== ይጽዳ ==click== መጫን ==client== ጠሪ ==client-server relationship== ጠሪ-ተጠሪ ግንኙነት ==clients== ጠሪዎች ==clip== መያዣ ==clipboard== መያዣ-ሰሌዳ ==clobber== ይምታ ==clock== ሰዓት ==clone== የተኮረጀ ==close (a)== ይዘጋ ==close== ይዘጋ ==closer== ጠጋ-ይበል ==closest== አጠገብ-ያለው ==code== ኮድ ==collaboration== ትብብር ==collapse== ውድቀት ==collate== በቅደም ተከተል ይደርድር ==collect e-mail== ኢmeልዕክ ይሰብሰብ ==collection== ስብስብ ==colon== ኮለን ==color capabilities== የቀለም

ችሎታ ==color== ቀለም ==colorspace== የቀለም-
ቦታ ==colour resolution== የቀለም ድምቀት
==column span== የዐምድ ስፋት ==column==
ዐምድ ==com port (communications port)==
የመገናኛ በር ==combination== ቅንጅት
==combine== ይቀናጅ ==combo box== ሁለገብ
ሳጥን ==comma== ኮማ ==command (n)== ትዕዛዝ
==command line (n)== ትዕዛዝ መስጫ ==command
line invocations== ትዕዛዝ መስጫ ማስነሳት
==command== ትዕዛዝ ==comment== አስተያየት
==common== ተራ ==company== ኩባንያ
==compare== ይመዛዝን ==compatibility==
መስማማት ==compatible== ተስማሚ ==compile==
ይቀናበር ==complete== ሙሉ ==complex==
ውስብስብ ==component== ክፍለ-ነገር
==compose== ይርቀቅ ==composer== ደራሲ
==compress== ይታመቅ ==compression== እመቃ
==computer== ኮምፒዩተር ==computer-literate==
ስለኮምፒዩተር የተማረ ==concatenate== ይያያዝ
==concatenations== ማያያዝ ==condense==
ይጥበብ ==condition== ቅድመ-ሁኔታ
==conditional== በቅድመ-ሁኔታ

configuration file

1. የማመቻቻ ስነድ

configuration utility

　　1. የማመቻቻ ፕሮግራም

configuration

　　1. ማመቻቸት

　　2. ማዋቀር

configure

　　1. አስተካክል

　　2. አመቻች

　　3. አዋቅር

　　4. አሰናዳ

　　5. አመቻች

　　6. ሙቅረት

　　7. መዋቅር

confirmation

　　1. መስማማት

　　2. ማረጋገጥ

conflict

1. ግጭት

connect to a server

1. ከተጠሪ ይገናኝ

connect

1. አገናኝ

connection failure

1. የማገናኘት መሰናከል

connection string

1. የግንኙነት ሐረግ

connection

1. ግንኙነት

connector

1. አገናኝ

constant

1. የማይቀየር

console

    1. መደብ

content

    1. ይዘት

context

    1. አግባብ

continue

    1. ይቀጥል

contrast

    1. ይነጻጸር

control (n)

    1. ቁጥጥር

control (v)

    1. ቁጥጥር ይደረግበት

control panel መቆጣጠሪያ ገበታ controller cards
ተቆጣጣሪ ካርዶች controls መቆጣጠርያዎች
conventional ተለምዷዊ converge መሰብሰብ
convergence መሰብሰብ conversion መለወጥ convert

ይለወጥ converter ለዋጭ cookie የቃኚ-ማስታወሻ coordinate ይቀነባበር copy ኮፒ copyright የኮፒ-መብት core ማዕከል correction እርማት corrupt የተበላሽ corrupted የተበላሽ count ይቆጠር counter ቆጣሪ country code የአገር ኮድ cover page ልባግድ cracker ሰባሪ crash ግጭት create links ጠቁሚ ይፈጠር create shortcut አቋራጭ ይፈጠር create ይፈጠር creator ፈጣሪ credentials መረጃ credits ተሳታፊዎች criteria ቅድመ-ሁኔታ criterium ቅድመ-ሁኔታ

critical

1. ወሳኝ

2. ሰባሪነፕብ

crop

1. ይቆረጥ

cross

1. መስቀል

cross-post (v) ተሻግሮ-ይላክ cross-posting አሻግሮ-መላክ crosshair pointer መስቀለኛ-አመልካች crossreference መስቀለኛ-አጣቃሽ cube አንኳር curly brackets ጥምልል ቅንፍ curly quotes ጥምልል ጥቅስ cursor ጠቋሚ curve ኩርባ custom ለተጠቃሚ-እንደሚመች-የተሰራ customize ለተጠቃሚ-እንደሚመች-ይስተካከል customized ለተጠቃሚ-

90

እንደሚመች-ተስተካክሷል cut ይቆረጥ cyan ሲያን cylinder ክብ-አምድ፡

Amharic Computer Glossary – D

- 1 daily
- 2 dark
- 3 dashed
- 4 day
- 5 deactivate
- 6 debug
- 7 debugger
- 8 decrease
- 9 Del (delete)
- 10 delay
- 11 design
- 12 details
- 13 diagonal
- 14 diagram
- 15 dictionary
- 16 distribute
- 17 divide
- 18 dropdown menu
- 19 duration
- 20 daemon
- 21 damage
- 22 data area

- 23 data bank
- 24 data bit
- 25 data
- 26 database
- 27 datasheet
- 28 date
- 29 deactivate
- 30 debug (n)
- 31 debug (v)
- 32 debugging
- 33 decimal numbers
- 34 decimal
- 35 direction
- 36 directory
- 37 disability
- 38 disable
- 39 disc
- 40 discard
- 41 disclaimer
- 42 disconnect
- 43 discussion board
- 44 discussion
- 45 disk capacity
- 46 disk space

- 47 disk
- 48 display (n)
- 49 display (v)
- 50 display class
- 51 displayed
- 52 disposition
- 53 document
- 54 documentation
- 55 dollar
- 56 domain
- 57 done
- 58 dots per inch
- 59 dotted line
- 60 double (v)
- 61 double-click
- 62 doubleclick
- 63 down (vi)
- 64 down (vt)
- 65 download
- 66 downtime
- 67 draft
- 68 drag and drop
- 69 drag
- 70 canvas

- 71 drawing object bar
- 72 drive
- 73 driver
- 74 drop
- 75 dropdown list
- 76 dual mode
- 77 dump (v)
- 78 dump
- 79 duplicate

daily

1. በየቀኑ

dark

1. ጨለማ

dashed

1. ባለሰረዝ

day

1. ቀን

deactivate

1. አቦዝን

debug

    1. ኢ.ተውሳክ (bug=ተውሳክ)

    2. መፈውስ

debugger

    1. ኢ.ተውሳክ (bug=ተውሳክ)

    2. መፈውስ

    3. ጸረ-ትኋን

decrease

    1. ይነስ

Del (delete)

    1. ይሰረዝ

delay

    1. ቆይታ

design

    1. ንድፍ

details

    1. ዝርዝሮች

diagonal

   1. አግድም

diagram

   1. የንድፍ ምስል

dictionary

   1. መዝገበ-ቃላት

distribute

   1. ይከፋፈል

divide

   1. ይካፈል

dropdown menu

   1. ተዘርጊ ምርጫ

duration

   1. ጊዜ

daemon

   1. ረጂ

damage

   1. ብልሽት

data area

   1. የመረጃ አካባቢ

data bank

   1. የመረጃ ባንክ

data bit

   1. የመረጃ-ቢት

data

   1. መረጃ

database

   1. መረጃ-ቤት

datasheet

   1. የመረጃ-ሥንጠረዥ

date

   1. ቀን

deactivate

1. አስተኛ

debug (n)

1. ተውሳክ ማስተካክል

debug (v)

1. ተውሳክ ይስተካከል

debugging

1. ተውሳክ-ማስተካከል

decimal numbers

1. ክፋይ ቁጥሮች

decimal

1. ክፋይ-ቁጥር

decision ውሳኔ decline አይቀበል decode ይፈታ
decoding መፍታት decompress ይዘርጋ
decompression መዘርጋት decrypt ይፈታ decryption
መፍታት dedicated የተመደበለት default gateway
ቀዳሚ መውጫ-በር default search engine ቀዳሚ አሳሽ
ሞተር default value ቀዳሚ እሴት default ቀዳሚ
define ይሰየም definition ፍቹ degree ደረጃ delegate
ይወክል delete ይስረዝ deleting በመሰረዝ ላይ deletion

99

ሰረዛ deletions ሰረዛዎች delimiter ከፋፋይ deliver (v) ይድረስ demo መሞከሪያ department ክፍል deprecated ረከሰ depth ጥልቀት descending ወራጅ description መግለጫ desktop የስራ-ሠሌዳ destination መድረሻ detail ዝርዝር detect ይገኝ detection ማግኘት developer አልሚ device independent ከማንኛውም ቂስ ጥገኝነት ነፃ የሆነ device manager ቂስ-አስተዳዳሪ device ቂስ diacritics አባባል-ገላጭ diagnostics ምርምር dial out (v) ይደወል dial tone የስልክ-ድምፅ dial ይደወል dial-up (adj) የስልክ dial-up (v) ይደወል dial-up networking የስልክ-መረብ dialog መልዕክት-መለዋወጥ dialogue box የመልዕክት-መለዋወጫ ሳጥን digit ቂጥር-ቤት digital camera ቂጥራዊ ካሜራ digital signature ቂጥራዊ-ፊርማ digital ቂጥራዊ dimension ልክ dimmed command ድብዝዝ ትዕዛዝ direction keys የአቅጣጫ ቂልፎች

direction

   1. አቅጣጫ

directory

   1. ዶሴ

disability

   1. ጉድለት

2. መስሳን

disable

1. አይቻል

2. ከልክል

disc

1. ካዝና

discard

1. ይወገድ

disclaimer

1. ካጅ

disconnect

1. ግንኙነት ይቋረጥ

discussion board

1. ውይይት መድረክ

discussion

1. ውይይት

disk capacity

   1. የካዝና-መጠን

disk space

   1. የካዝና ቦታ

disk

   1. ካዝና

display (n)

   1. ማሳያ

   2. ማይ

display (v)

   1. ይታይ

display class

   1. የማሳያ ትዕዛዝ ክፍል

displayed

   1. ይታያል

disposition

   1. ባህርይ

document

   1. ሰነድ

documentation

   1. መመሪያ

dollar

   1. ዶላር

domain

   1. ክባቢ

done

   1. አልቋል

dots per inch

   1. ነጥቦች በኢንች ውስጥ

   2. ነበኢ (ነጥብ በ በኢንች)

dotted line

   1. ነጠብጣ መስመር

double (v)

   1. ደርብ

2. ይደረብ

double-click

1. ሁለቴ-ተጫን

2. ሁለቴ-ይጫን

doubleclick

1. ሁለቴ-ተጫን

2. ሁለቴ-ይጫን

down (vi)

1. ወደታች

down (vt)

1. ወደታች

download

1. አምጣ

2. ይምጣ

3. አውርድ

downtime

1. ድኩምጊዜ

2. ሥራፈት-ጊዜ

draft

1. ንድፍ

drag and drop

1. ነትቶ መጣል

2. ነትተህ ጣል

drag

1. ነትት

2. ይነተት

canvas

1. ምንጣፍ

drawing object bar

1. የስዕል-መሣሪያዎች-ማስጫ

drive

1. ማጫወቻ (cd, flopy...etc)

2. ማንደC (hard drive)

3. ካዝና (hard drive)

driver

1. ማጫወቻ (media drivers, cd flopy)

2. ነጂ (device drivers)

drop

1. ተሸብላይ (dropdown menu=ተሸብላይ ምናሌ)

2. ተዘርጊ

dropdown list

1. ተሸብላይ ዝርዝር

2. ተዘርጊ ዝርዝር

dual mode

1. ባለ ሁለት ፀባይ

2. ፀባየ ሁለት

dump (v)

1. ጥርቅም ውስጥ ይጨመር

dump

1. ጥርቅም

duplicate

1. አባዛ

dynamic IP-address ተለዋዋጭ የኢንተርኔት ወግ አድራሻ

Amharic Computer Glossary – E

- 1 edition
- 2 empty
- 3 envelope
- 4 equation
- 5 Esc (escape)
- 6 ethernet
- 7 encrypted text
- 8 encryption
- 9 evaluation
- 10 event
- 11 events
- 12 exactly
- 13 exclamation point
- 14 exclusive
- 15 executable file(s)
- 16 executable program
- 17 execution
- 18 exist
- 19 existing
- 20 exit buttons

- 21 exit
- 22 expand (an outline)
- 23 expand
- 24 explore
- 25 explorer
- 26 export
- 27 express
- 28 expression
- 29 extend
- 30 extension
- 31 external
- 32 extract

edition

1. ሕትመት

empty

1. ባዶ

envelope

1. ፖስታ

equation

1. እኩልታ

e-mail ኢ-መልዕክት echo ይስተጋባ edit (the action) ይታረም (ድርጊት) edit (the button) ይታረም (ቁልፍ) editor አራሚ effect ክንዉን eject ይዉጣ electronic mail የኤሌክትሮኒክ-መልዕክት element መሠረተ-ነገር ellipsis ቃለ-ነደሎ email ኤመልዕክት embedded ተለጣፊ emoticon የስሜት-ምልክት emulator ኮራጅ enable ይቻል enclose ይሽፈን encode ኮድ-ይጻፍ encoding የሆሄያት ኮድ

Esc (escape)

1. የመውጫ መጥሪያ

ethernet

1. ኤተርኔት

every ሁሉም example ምሳሌ exception በስተቀር explain ያስረዳል

encrypted text

1. የኮድ ጽሑፍ

2. የመሰጠረ ጽሑፍ

3. የተመሰጠረ ጽሑፍ

encrypted በኮድ-የተገፈ

encryption

1. በኮድ-መጻፍ

2. ማመስጠር

end መጨረሻ enhance ይጨምር enhanced
የተጨመረለት enter (n) መላሽ-ቁልፍ enter (v) መልስ
entry መግቢያ envelope orientation የፖስታ
አቀማመጥ environment variable የከባቢ-ተለዋዋጭ
environment ከባቢ equal sign እኩል ይሆናል ምልክት
erase ይደምስስ error message የስህተት መልዕክት
error ስህተት evaluate ይገምግም

evaluation

1. ግምገማ

2. ዋጋ መስጠት

event

1. ክንውን

2. ድርጊት

events

1. ክንውኖች

exactly

1. በትክክል

exclamation point

1. የቃለ-አጋኖ ነጥብ

exclusive

1. አግላይ

2. ውሱን

3. ብቸኛ

executable file(s)

1. ፈፃሚ-ሰነድ

2. ገባሪ

executable program

1. ፈፃሚ-ፕሮግራም

2. ገባሪ ስልት

==execute==

1. አስኪድ

2. ተግብር

execution

    1. ማስፈጸም

    2. መግበር

exist

    1. ነዋሪ

    2. ኗሪ

    3. ይኑር

existing

    1. ያለ

    2. የነበረ

exit buttons

    1. የይውጣ-ቁልፎች

exit

    1. ውጣ

expand (an outline)

    1. ይስፋ

    2. አስፋ

expand

1. ይስፋ

2. አስፋ

explore

1. ቃኝ

2. ፈትሽ

3. በርብር

explorer

1. የማይክሮሶፍት ቃኚ

export

1. ላክ

2. ስደድ

3. ለውጥ

express

1. ይገለጽ

2. ግለጽ

expression

    1. አገላለጽ

    2. ገላጭ

    3. መግለጫ

extend

    1. ይርዘም

    2. አርዝም

extension

    1. ቅጥያ

    2. ማራዘሚያ

external

    1. ውጫያዊ

extract

    1. አውጣጣ

    2. ጭመቅ

Amharic Computer Glossary – F

- 1 FAQ (Frequently Asked Questions)
- 2 FAQ
- 3 FYI (For Your Information)
- 4 failure
- 5 fill
- 6 firewall
- 7 first
- 8 flip
- 9 flowchart
- 1 FAQ (Frequently Asked Questions)
- 2 FAQ
- 3 FYI (For Your Information)
- 4 failure
- 5 fill
- 6 firewall
- 7 first
- 8 flip
- 9 flowchart

FAQ (Frequently Asked Questions)

1. ተደጋጋሚ ጥያቄዎች

FAQ

1. ተደጋጋሚ ጥያቄዎች

FYI (For Your Information)

1. እንዲያውቁት

failure

1. መሰሰናከል

fill

1. ሙላ

firewall

1. የሳትግምብ

first

1. አንደኛ

flip

1. ይገልበጥ

follow Up ይከታተኂል from ከ front ፊት Full screen
ሙሉ ስክሪን face type የፊደል-ቅርጽ አይነት fail
ብልሽት failure ብልሽት false ውሸት fast ቶሎ favorite
ተመራጭ favourite ተመራጭ fax ፋክስ feature ገጽታ
feedback ምላሽ field መደብ file transfer protocol
(FTP) ሰነድ ማስተላለፊያ ወግ file ሰነድ filter (n) አጣሪ
filter (v) ይጣራ find ይፈልግ finish ይፈፅም firewall
የእሳት-አጥር first name ስም fit ይመጠን fix ይጠገን
flag ባንዲራ flags ባንዲራዎች floating ተንሳፋፊ
floppy disk ፍሎፒ-ካዝና flow control የፈሰስ
መቆጣጠሪያ

flowchart

1. የቅደም-ተከተል-ንድፍ

2. የሂድት ዱካ

focus ማነጣጠር folder ዶሴ font የፊደል ቅርጽ
==footer== የገጽ ግርጌ ==footnote== የግርጌ-
ማስታወሻ foreground የፊት-ገፅታ feed ማጉረስ form
ቅፅ format (n) ማዘጋጀት format (v) ይዘጋጅ
formatting ማዘጋጀት formula ፎርሙላ forum
መድረክ forward slash ወደፊት-ያዘነበለ-መስመር
forward ወደፊት fourheaded arrow በለ አራት-ራስ
ቀስት fraction ክፋይ frame ክልል frameset ክልል
framework ክልል free (to ~ up space on disk) ቦታ-
ማስለቀቅ (ካዝና ውስጥ) freeware ነፃ-ፕሮግራም freeze
ይቄም frequency ድግግሞሽ Frequently Asked
Questions በተደጋጋሚ የሚጠየቁ ጥያቄዎች frontend

የፊት ==frontslash== ፊትአዝማሚ, ቀኝአዝማሚ full-screen mode ሙሉ-ስክሪን function ተግባር

Amharic Computer Glossary – G

- 1 gallery
- 2 game(s)
- 3 gateway
- 4 general
- 5 graph

gallery

   1. የስዕል-አዳራሽ

game(s)

   1. ጨዋታ(ዎች)

gateway

   1. መውጫ-በር

general

   1. አጠቃላይ

gigabyte ጊጋባይት global ሁሉ-አቀፍ glossary
መድበለ-ቃል go ይሂድ gradient ለውጥ grammar
ሰዋሰው grant permission ይፈቀድ

graph

1. ሠንጠረዥ

graphic

1. ሠንጠረዥዊ

2. ስዕላዊ

graphics

1. የሠንጠርዥ ሥራ

2. የስዕል ሰራ

greater than ይበልጣል greeting ሰላምታ grid መረብ
group ቡድን grouping ቡድን-ምስረታ guest እንግዳ
guideline ደንብ guide መመሪያ

Amharic Computer Glossary – H

- 1 Help File
- 2 high
- 3 hacker
- 4 handheld
- 5 handle
- 6 handout
- 7 handshake
- 8 handwriting
- 9 hang (v)
- 10 hang up
- 11 hard drive - disk
- 12 hardcopy
- 13 harddisk
- 14 hardware
- 15 hash
- 16 header
- 17 heading
- 18 height
- 19 help
- 20 hidden
- 21 hide
- 22 highlight (v)

- 23 highlight (n)
- 24 home page
- 25 home
- 26 horizontal
- 27 host
- 28 hotkey
- 29 hour
- 30 hourglass
- 31 hyperlink
- 32 hypertext
- 33 hyphen
- 34 hyphenation

Help File

1. መመሪያ ሰነድ

high

1. ከፍ

hacker

1. ሀከር

handheld

   1. በእጅ-የሚያዝ

handle

   1. እጀታ

handout

   1. ምጽዋት

handshake

   1. መጨበጥ

handwriting

   1. የእጅ-ጽሑፍ

hang (v)

   1. ይሰቀል

hang up

   1. ይዘጋ

hard drive - disk

   1. ካዝና

   2. ማጓደር

hardcopy

1. በወረቀት የታተመ ቅጂ

harddisk

1. ካዝና

hardware

1. ጥጥር አካል (software=ልስልስ አካል)

hash

1. ሰረዝ

2. አራት ማዕዘን (key)

3. ቀመር (programing)

header

1. የእናት ማስታወሻ

heading

1. አርእስት

height

1. ቁመት

help

1. መመሪያ

2. rdata

hidden

1. የተደበቀ

2. dbq

hide

1. ይደበቅ

2. debiq

highlight (v)

1. ይጉላ

2. agula

highlight (n)

1. yegola

2. ማጉላት

highlighter አጉሊ hint ፍንጭ history ታሪክ hit ምት
hold ይያዝ home button የቤት ቁልፍ home directory
የቤት ዶሴ

home page

   1. mereb bet

   2. የቤት ገጽ

home

   1. ቤት

horizontal

   1. አግድም

host

   1. ተጠሪ

   2. አገልጋይ

   3. አስተናጋጅ

hotkey

   1. ቁልፍ

hour

   1. ሰዓት

hourglass

   1. የሰዓት-ጠርሙስ

hyperlink

1. አንዳኝ

hypertext

1. ተንዳኝ-ሰነድ

hyphen

1. ሰረዝ

hyphenation

1. በሰረዝ-ማያያዝ

2. ቃል-እያያዠ

3. ቃል-አቆራኝ

Amharic Computer Glossary – I

- 1 I/O (input/output)
- 2 ID
- 3 interface
- 4 IP (Internet Protocol)
- 5 ISP (Internet Service Provider)
- 6 ISP
- 7 ignore

I/O (input/output)

1. ግባት/ውጤት

ID

1. መለያ

interface

1. በይነገጽ

IP (Internet Protocol)

1. ኢንተርኔት ፕሮቶኮል(ኢፕ)

2. ኢንተርኔት ወግ

ISP (Internet Service Provider)

   1. የኢንተርኔት አገልግሎት ሰጪ.

ISP

   1. የኢንተርኔት አገልግሎት ሰጪ.

ignore

   1. ይተዉ.

importance እስፈላጊነት increase ይተልቅ initials
ፊርማ international አለም-አቀፋዊ Internet ኢንተርኔት
icon ምልክት identifier ጠቋሚ idle (n) ሥራ-ፈት
image ምስል import ይምጣ inactive የማይንቀሳቀስ
inbox መጪ.-መልዕክቶች incoming መጪ.
incompatible የማይስማማ inconsistency የመለዋወጥ-
ፀባይ inconsistent ተለዋዋጭ incorrect የተሳሳተ
indent (v) አዲስ አንቀጽ መጀመር indent (n) አዲስ
አንቀጽ index ማውጫ indicator ጠቋሚ info መመሪያ
information መመሪያ infrared ኢንፍራሬድ-ጨረር
initialize ይንቅሳቀስ ink ቀለም inner margin የውስጥ
ህዳግ input box የግባት ሳጥን input ግባት insert cells
down ሳጥኖች በመሃል ይግቡ insert ይክተት insertion
መክተት install ይተከል installation ተከላ instance
ክስተት instruction መመሪያ integer ሙሉብጥ-ቁጥር
integrated የተጣመረ integrity ፅኑነት interactive
ተቀባባይ interface ገፅታ internal የውስጥ interrupt
ይቋረጥ intranet ውስጣዊ-መረብ invalid የማይሰራ

130

invert ይገልበጥ invisible የማይታይ invite ይጋበዝ
italic ያዘመመ item ዕቃ iteration ድግግሞሽ

Amharic Computer Glossary – J

- 1 Javascript
- 2 jammed
- 3 job
- 4 jobs (e.g. print jobs)
- 5 join
- 6 journal
- 7 jump
- 8 junk mail
- 9 justification
- 10 justified
- 11 Justify

Javascript

1. የጃባ-ድርሰት

jammed

1. ተቀርቅሯል

job

1. ስራ

jobs (e.g. print jobs)

   1. ሰራዎች

join

   1. ይቀላቀል

journal

   1. ማስታወሻ

jump

   1. ይዘለል

junk mail

   1. የማይጠቅም-መልዕክት

justification

   1. ምክንያት

justified

   1. መስመሮች እኩል እንዲሆኑ ቃላትን ማጠጋጋት

Justify

   1. አሰልፍ

Amharic Computer Glossary – K

- 1 keep track
- 2 keep
- 3 key (on keyboard)
- 4 keyboard
- 5 keypad
- 6 keyword
- 7 kilobyte
- 8 kit

keep track
1.　ክትትል ይደረግበት
keep
1.　ይያዝ
key (on keyboard)
1.　ቁልፍ (ቁልፍ-ገበታ ላይ)
keyboard
1.　የቁልፍ-ገበታ
keypad
1.　የቁልፍ-ገበታ
keyword
1.　ቁልፍ ቃል

kilobyte

    1.   ኪሎባይት

kit

    1.   ስንቅ

Amharic Computer Glossary – L

- 1 LAN (local area network)
- 2 large
- 3 layout
- 4 length
- 5 linear
- 6 label
- 7 language
- 8 laptop
- 9 link
- 10 load
- 11 local network
- 12 locale
- 13 location
- 14 lock
- 15 log (v)
- 16 log file
- 17 log in
- 18 log off

LAN (local area network)

    1.   የቅርብ አካባቢ መረጃ መረብ

large

    1.   ትልቅ

layout

    1.   አጣጣል

length

    1.   ርዝመት

linear

    1.   የመስመር

label

    1.   መለያ

landscape

    1.   አግድም

language

    1.   ቋንቋ

laptop

    1.   የጉዞ-ኮምፒተር

last modified መጨረሻ የተሻሻለው last visited መጨረሻ የተጎበኘው launch ይጀምር layer ምንጣፍ layout table የገድፍ ሠንጠረዥ layout ገድፍ leading መምራት less ያነሰ level ደረጃ library ረዳት-ፕሮግራሞች license ፈቃድ agreement ስምምነት line

break መስመር መለያ line መስመር link (to) አገናኝ
(ከ...ጋር)

link

1. አገናኝ

2. መያያዝ

list

1. ዝርዝር

load

1. ይምጣ(ይምጣ)

2. ይጫን(ትዕዛዝ)

3. ጫን(ግስ)

4. ጭነት(ስም)

local network

1. የእካባቢ መረጃ መረብ

2. የቅርብ መረጃ መረብ

locale

1. እካባቢ

2. ቅርብ

location

1. ቦታ

2. ማደሪያ

lock

    1.   ይቆለፍ፡

log (v)

    1.   ሎግ (ግስ)

    2.   የመግቢያ-ማስታወሻ-ይፃፍ

log file

    1.   የሎግ ሰነድ

    2.   ማስታወሻ

log in

    1.   ሎግ ግባ

    2.   ይገባል

log off

    1.   ሎግ አጥፋ

    2.   ዘግተው ይወጣል

=log on= ሎግ አድርግ፤ ይገባል =log out= ሎግ ውጣ፤ ዘግተው ይወጣል =log (n)= የመግቢያ-ማስታወሻ =logarithm= ሎጋሪዝም =logging= መግባት =logical= ሎጂካዊ =login (info)= የመግቢያ-ማስታወቂያ =logo= አርማ =look up= ይመልከት =loop = ዞር-ገጠም =loudspeaker= ድምፅ-ማጉያ =low= ዝቅ =lowercase= ትንሹ-የላቲን-ፊደላት

Amharic Computer Glossary – M

- 1 magnifier
- 2 managed (wierless network)
- 3 master (as in hard diks)
- 4 merge
- 5 middle
- 6 more
- 7 macro
- 8 mailbox
- 9 mailing list
- 10 manager
- 11 manual
- 12 margin
- 13 mark
- 14 mask
- 15 master
- 16 match
- 17 matrix
- 18 matte
- 19 maximise
- 20 maximize
- 21 mean
- 22 measure

- 23 measurement
- 24 media
- 25 memory
- 26 menu bar
- 27 menu
- 28 menu button
- 29 menu item
- 30 merge
- 31 message
- 32 method
- 33 microphone
- 34 microprocessor
- 35 minimise
- 36 minimize
- 37 module
- 38 monitor (n)
- 39 monitor (v)
- 40 mount
- 41 mount point
- 42 mouse pad
- 43 mouse
- 44 mousewheel
- 45 move (v)
- 46 multilingual

- 47 multimedia
- 48 multiple recipient
- 49 multiple selection
- 50 multiuser
- 51 mute

magnifier
>   1.   አጉሊ.

managed (wireless network)
>   1.   ቀጥታ

(see adhoc)

master (as in hard diks)
>   1.   ቀዳሚ (slave=ተከታይ)
>   2.   ዋና
>   3.   ጌታ

merge
>   1.   ይቀላቀል
>   2.   አቀላቅል

middle
>   1.   መሀከል

more
>   1.   ተጨማሪ

macro

    1.   ንዑስ ትዕዛዝ

mailbox

    1.   ፖስታ-ሳጥን

mailing list

    1.   መልዕክት መቀባበያ ማዕከል

manager

    1.   አስተዳዳሪ

manual

    1.   መመሪያ

margin

    1.   ህዳግ

mark

    1.   ምልክት

mask

    1.   መሸፈኛ

master

    1.   ዋና

match

    1.   ይመሳሰል

matrix

    1.   ሜትሪክስ

matte

    1.   ደብዛዛ

maximise

    1.   አተልቅ

    2.   ይተልቅ

maximize

    1.   አተልቅ

    2.   ይተልቅ

mean

    1.   መዕከላዊ

measure

    1.   ይለካ

    2.   ለካ

measurement

    1.   መለኪያ

media

    1.   መገናኛ

    2.   ማህደረመረጃ

medium ማዕከል megabyte (MB) ሜጋባይት (ሜባ)

member አባል memo ማስታወሻ

memory

    1.   አስታዋሽ

    2.   ማህደረትውስታ

    3.   ማህደር

menu bar

    1.   ምርጫ ማስጫ

    2.   ምናልሌ(ምናሌ) አሞሌ

menu proxies የምርጫ-ምስለኔ

menu

    1.   ምርጫ

    2.   ምናልሌ (ምናሌ)

menu button

    1.   ምናሌ አዝራር

menu item

    1.   ምናሌ ነገር

merge

    1.   መግጠም

message

    1.   መልዕክት

method

    1.   ዘዴ

microphone

    1.   መነጋገሪያ

    2.   ድምፅ ማጉያ

microprocessor

    1.   አስሊ

minimise

    1.   ይነስ

    2.   አሳንስ

minimize

    1.   ይነስ

    2.   አሳንስ

minimum በትንሹ minus sign የመቀነስ ምልክት
mirror (v) ያስተጋባ mirror አስተጋቢ miscellaneous
ልዩልዩ mismatch (v) አይመሳሰል mix ይደባለቅ mode
የአሠራር ዘዴ model ሞዴል modem (modulator-
demodulator) ሞደም moderated የሚስተናበር
modify ይለወጥ

module

    1.   ክፍል

monitor (n)

    1.   መመልከቻ

monitor (v)

    1.   ክትትል ይደረግ

mount

    1.   ጫን

mount point

    1.   የመጫኛ ጣቢያ

mouse pad

    1.   የጠቋሚ ምንጣፍ

    2.   የአይጥ ምንጣፍ

mouse

    1.   ጠቋሚ

    2.   አይጥ

mousewheel

    1.   የጠቋሚ-መዘውር

    2.   የአይጥ-መዘውር

    3.   የአይጥ-መሪ

move (v)

    1.   ያሂድ

    2.   ሂድ

multilingual

    1.   ቋንቋ-ብዙ

    2.   ልሳነ-ብዙ

multimedia

    1.   ባሕርይ-ብዙ-መገናኛ

    2.   ብዝሃ ማጎደረ-መረጃ

multiple recipient

1. ብዙ ተቀባይ
2. ተቀባየ ·ብዙ

multiple selection

1. ብዙ ምርጫ
2. ምርጫ ·ብዙ

multiuser

1. ተጠቃሚ.-ብዙ

mute

1. ድምፅ-አልባ
2. ድምፅ-ከል

Amharic Computer Glossary – N

- 1 NUM LOCK key
- 2 n/a
- 3 name server
- 4 name
- 5 navigate
- 6 navigation
- 7 network
- 8 new
- 9 news

NUM LOCK key

    1.   የቁጥር-መጥሪያዎችን-ማስነሻ-ቁልፍ

n/a

    1.   አልተገኘም

name server

    1.   ስም አገልጋይ

    2.   ስም ተጠሪ

name

    1.   ስም

navigate

    1.   ቃኝ

navigation

    1.   መቃኘት

network

    1.   መረብ

    2.   አውታC

new

    1.   አዲስ

news

    1.   ዜና

newsgroup የዜና-ቡድን newsletter የዜና-መፅሔት next የሚቀጥለው nickname ቅጽል ስም no አይ node አንጓ non-blank ባዶ-ያልሆነ-ነጽ none ምንም normal የተለመደ not writeable መጻፍ-አይፈቀድም note ማስታወሻ notify ያሳውቅ number ቁጥC numbered ቁጥC የተሰጠው numbering ቁጥC አሰጣጥ

Amharic Computer Glossary – O

- 1 OK
- 2 old
- 3 other
- 4 object
- 5 objects
- 6 off
- 7 office
- 8 offline (go)

OK

    1.   እሽ

old

    1.   አርጌ

    2.   ያረጀ

other

    1.   ሌላ

object

    1.   ነገር

objects

    1.   ነገሮች

1. ይጥፋ

office

1. ቢሮ

offline (go)

1. ከመስመር-ውጪ. (ሂድ)

offline ከመስመር-ውጪ. offset ይመዝን omit ይቅር on ይብራ online መስመር-ላይ open software localization project ክፍት የፕሮግራም ትርጉም ፕሮጀክት open source ክፍት-ስልት open ይከፈት operating system ገቢ-ስልት operation(s) ተግባር operation ተግባር operator ነጃ optimize ይሻሻል option ምርጫ optional ተመራጭ organise ይደራጅ organzation ድርጅት orientation አቀማመጥ original ቀዳማይ outbox የወጪ.-መልዕክቶች-ሳጥን outer margin የታችኛው ህዳግ outgoing message ወጪ. መልዕክት outline ገፅታ output ውጤት overlap ተደራራቢ override መብቱ-ይነጠቅ overwrite(v) ተሰርዞ ይጻፍ owner ባለቤት ownership ባለቤትነት

Amharic Computer Glossary – P

- 1 PAGE DOWN key
- 2 PAGE UP key
- 3 passphrase
- 4 PAUSE key
- 5 PC
- 6 PRINT SCRN key
- 7 pattern
- 8 play
- 9 polygon
- 10 probabilit
- 11 profession
- 12 professional
- 13 protection
- 14 Public Domain Software
- 15 pyramid
- 16 page break
- 17 page orientation
- 18 page setup
- 19 page
- 20 paginate
- 21 pagination
- 22 palette

- 23 pane
- 24 panel
- 25 paper bin
- 26 paper jam
- 27 paper
- 28 paragraph
- 29 parallel
- 30 parameter
- 31 parent (hierarchy)
- 32 parenthesis
- 33 parity
- 34 partition
- 35 parser
- 36 password
- 37 paste
- 38 patch
- 39 path
- 40 plug in (v)
- 41 plug-in (n)
- 42 plus sign
- 43 point (v)
- 44 point
- 45 pointer
- 46 Point-to-Point

- 47 policy
- 48 popup (n)
- 49 popup (v)
- 50 port
- 51 portrait
- 52 position
- 53 positioning
- 54 post
- 55 postal code
- 56 power
- 57 predefined
- 58 preference
- 59 preferences
- 60 prefix
- 61 prepare
- 62 preset
- 63 press
- 64 preview
- 65 primary
- 66 print job
- 67 print
- 68 program
- 69 protocol

PAGE DOWN key

   1.   የገጽ-ወደታች ቁልፍ

PAGE UP key

   1.   የገጽ-ወደላይ ቁልፍ

passphrase

   1.   ማለፊያ ቃል

PAUSE key

   1.   የቆም-ይበል ቁልፍ

PC

   1.   አሰሊ

PRINT SCRN key

   1.   ስክሪኑን-አትም ቁልፍ

package ጥቅል Page view ገጽ ማሳያ personal የግል

pattern

   1.   ጥለት

   2.   ሰርዓተ ጥለት

play

   1.   ተጫወት

   2.   ይጫወቱ

   1.   ይጫወቷል

polygon

   1.   መድብለገጽ

   2.   ባለ ብዙ ጎን ማዕዘን

probabilit

    1.   የመሆን-እድል

profession

    1.   ሙያ

professional

    1.   ባለሙያ

protection

    1.   ጥበቃ

Public Domain Software

    1.   የሕዝብ-ጥቅም ፕሮግራም

pyramid

    1.   ፒራሚድ

page break

    1.   የገጽ መቁረጫ

page orientation

    1.   የገጽ አቀማመጥ

page setup

    1.   የገጽ ቅንጅት

page

    1.   ገጽ

paginate

    1.   የገጽ-ቁጥር-ይስጥ

pagination

1.   የገጽ-ቀፕር አሰጣፕ

palette

1.   የቀለም-ገበታ

pane

1.   የመስኮት-መስተዋት

panel

1.   ገበታ

paper bin

1.   ወረቀት-ዘገቢል

paper jam

1.   ወረቀት-ጎርሻል

paper

1.   ወረቀት

paragraph

1.   ምዕራፍ

2.   አንቀጽ

parallel

1.   ትይዩ

parameter

1.   ግቤት

2.   ወሳኝ-እሴት

parent (hierarchy)

1.   ወላጅ

158

parenthesis

    1.   ቅንፍ

parity

    1.   ዝምድና

partition

    1.   ክፋይ

parser

    1.   ዘርዛሪ

password

    1.   ማለፊያ-ቃል

    2.   ሚስጥር-ቃል

paste

    1.   ለጥፍ

    2.   ይለጠፍ

patch

    1.   ልጥፍ

path

    1.   መንገድ

pattern ንድፍ pause እረፍት pen ብዕር percentage ከመቶ-እጅ performance ብቃት period ጊዜ permission (s) ፈቃድ personal computer ኮምፒተር pick ይመረጥ picture ሥዕል pie ተከፋይ pixel ፒክስል pixels ፒክስሎች placeholder ቦታ-ያዢ plain text ቀላል ጽሑፍ platform ገጺ-ሰልት plot area ቦታ ይሳል

plug in (v)

    1.   ይቀጥል

    2.   ሰካ

    3.   ይሰካ

plug-in (n)

    1.   ተቀጣይ

    2.   ተሰኪ

plus sign

    1.   የመደመር ምልክት

point (v)

    1.   ይጠቆም

point

    1.   ነጥብ

pointer

    1.   ጠቋሚ

Point-to-Point

    ከነጥብ-ነጥብ (p2p=ከነነ?)

policy

    1.   መርሃ-ግብር

    2.   ፖሊሲ

popup (n)

    1.   ፖፕባይ

popup (v)

    1.   ፖፕ ይበል

    2.   ፖፕ በል

port

    1.   በር

portrait

    1.   ቁም

position

    1.   የተቀመጠበት-ቦታ

positioning

    1.   አቀማመጥ

post

    1.   መልዕክት

postal code

    1.   የፖስታ ኮድ

power

    1.   ኃይል

predefined

    1.   ቀድሞ-የተወሰነ

preference

    1.   ምርጫ

preferences

    1.   ምርጫዎች

prefix

    1.   ባዕድ መነሻ

prepare

    1.   ይዘጋጅ

    2.   አዘጋጅ

preset

    1.   ቅድሞ-የተሰየመ

press

    1.   ይጫኑ

preview

    1.   ቅድሞ ማየ

primary

    1.   መጀመሪያ

print job

    1.   የህትመት ስራ

print

    1.   አትም

    2.   ይታተም

printer driver ማተሚያው-ነጂ printer ማተሚያ
priority ቅድሚያ privacy ገበና procedure ቅደም-
ተከተል process ሂደት processing በሂደት-ላይ product
ምርት profile ግለ-መግለጫ

program

1. ፕሮግራም

2. ስልት

progress ሂደት project የስራ-እቅድ promote ከፍ-ይበል prompt ያስነሳ properties ፀባዮች property ፀባይ protect ጥበቃ ይደረግለት

protocol

1. ፕሮቶኮል

2. ወግ

proxy server አስመሳይ ተጠሪ pt ነጥብ publication ኅትመት publish ይታተም

Amharic Computer Glossary – Q

- 1 quick
- 2 query (v)
- 3 query (n)
- 4 question mark
- 5 questions and answers
- 6 queue (n)
- 7 queue (v)
- 8 quit
- 9 quotation mark

quick

    1.   በፍጥነት

query (v)

    1.   ይጠየቅ

    2.   ጠይቅ

query (n)

    1.   መጠይቅ

question mark

    1.   የጥያቄ ምልክት

questions and answers

    1.   ጥያቄና መልስ

queue (n)

    1.   ሰልፍ

queue (v)

    1.   ይሰለፍ

quit

    1.   ይውጣ

    2.   ውጣ

quotation mark

    1.   የጥቅስ ምልክት

Amharic Computer Glossary – R

- 1 raid
- 2 radio button
- 3 RAM
- 4 random
- 5 re
- 6 range
- 7 reply
- 8 README file
- 9 RGB
- 10 recalculate
- 11 rectangle
- 12 redial
- 13 Ref:
- 14 region
- 15 reject
- 16 ribbon
- 17 Roman
- 18 read only
- 19 read
- 20 readability
- 21 rearrange
- 22 reboot

- 23 recall
- 24 receive
- 25 refresh
- 26 register (n)
- 27 register (v)
- 28 registration
- 29 reinstall
- 30 relation
- 31 relationship
- 32 release notes
- 33 release
- 34 reliable
- 35 reload
- 36 replace
- 37 replica
- 38 replication
- 39 reply
- 40 report
- 41 repository
- 42 requirement
- 43 reset
- 44 resize
- 45 reserved
- 46 resolution

- 47 resource
- 48 response
- 49 restart
- 50 restore
- 51 result
- 52 resume
- 53 retrieve
- 54 retry
- 55 root
- 56 rotate
- 57 round brackets
- 58 route
- 59 router
- 60 row
- 61 rule
- 62 ruler
- 63 rules
- 64 run

raid

1. የዲስክ በረከት

radio button

1. ራዲዮ ቁልፍ

RAM

    1.   ግትር ዲስክ

random

    1.   ነሲብ

    2.   አቦሰጥ

re

    1.   እንደገና

    2.   መልስ

range

    1.   መጠን

rate ፍጀታ

reply

    1.   ምላሽ

README file

    1.   ያንብቡኝ ሰነድ

RGB

    1.   ቀአሰ (ቀይ አረንጓዴ ሰማያዊ)

recalculate

    1.   እንደገና-ይሰላ

    2.   እንደገና-ይሰላ

rectangle

    1.   አራት ማዕዘን

redial

    1.   እንደገና ደውል

    2.   እንደገና-ይደወል

Ref:

    1.   ተጠቃሽ፦

region

    1.   አካባቢ

reject

    1.   አትቀበል

    2.   ከልክል

    3.   አይቀበል

ribbon

    1.   ሪባን

Roman

    1.   ሮማዊ

read only

    1.   የሚነበብ ብቻ

    2.   ንባብ-ብቻ

read

    1.   አንብብ

    2.   ይነበብ

readability

    1.   ተነባቢነት

rearrange

    1.   እንደገና-ይስተካከል

reboot

    1.   እንደገና አስነሳ

    2.   እንደገና ይነሳ

recall

    1.   ተመልሶ-ይጠራ

    2.   መልሰህ ጥራ

receive

    1.   ተቀበል

    2.   ይቀበሏል

recipient ተቀባይ record ይመዘገብ recover ይገኝ
recycle bin የቆሻሻ-ዘንቢል redirection ወደሌላ-ይላክ
redo እንደገና ይደረግ reduce ይቀነስ reference
ማጣቀሻ

refresh

    1.   አድስ

    2.   ይታደስ

register (n)

    1.   መዝገብ

register (v)

    1.   ይመዝገቡ

    2.   ተመዝገብ

registration

    1.   ምዝገባ

reinstall

    1.   እንደገና ይተከል

relation

    1.   ግንኙነት

relationship

    1.   ግንኙነት

release notes

    1.   የማቅረቢያ መልዕክት

    2.   የማስተዋወቂያ መልዕክት

    3.   የመልቀቂያ-መልዕክት

release

    1.   መልቀቅ (ግስ)

    2.   ማስተዋወቅ (ግስ)

    3.   አቅርቦት (ስም)

reliable

    1.   ታማኝ

    2.   የሚታመን

reload

    1.   እንደገና ጫን

    2.   እንደገና ይጫን

reminder አስታዋሽ remote ከርቀት remove
ይወገድ rename እንደገና ይሰየም repaginate
እንደገና-የገጽ-ቁጥር-ይሰጥ repair ይጠገን repeat
ይደገም repetition ድግግሞሽ

replace

    1.   ተካ

    2.   ይተካ

replica

    1.   ቅጂ

replication

    1.   መቅዳት

reply

    1.   መልስ

report

    1.   ሪፖርት

repository

    1.   ካዝና

    2.   ማኅደር

requirement

    1.   የግድ-አስፈላጊ

reset

    1.   እንደነበረ ይመለስ

resize

1. እንደገና መጠኑ ይስተካከል

reserved
1. የተከለለ

resolution
1. ድምቀት

resource
1. ንብረት
2. ጥሬ-መነሻ

response
1. መልስ

restart
1. እንደገና ይጀመር
2. እንደገና ጀምር

restore
1. እንደነበረ ይመለስ

result
1. ውጤት

resume
1. የቆመው ይቀጥል

retrieve
1. ይምጣ

retry
1. እንደገና ይሞከር

return ይመለስ retype እንደገና ይተየብ

review ግምገማ rights መብቶች role ሚና

root

    1.   ስር

    2.   ዋና

rotate

    1.   አዙር

    2.   ያዙር

round brackets

    1.   ክብ ቅንፍ

route

    1.   ያቀብሷል

    2.   አሰወጣ

router

    1.   አቀባይ

    2.   አሰወጪ

row

    1.   ረድፍ

rule

    1.   ደንብ

ruler

    1.   ማስመሪያ

rules

1. ደንቦች

run

1. ሂድ
2. ተግብር

Amharic Computer Glossary – S

- 1 SCROLL LOCK key
- 2 SHIFT key
- 3 SQL
- 4 scheme
- 5 sequence
- 6 sensor
- 7 serial
- 8 serie
- 9 server
- 10 Service
- 11 Service Pack
- 12 set
- 13 shading
- 14 sharing
- 15 shell
- 16 side
- 17 spacing
- 18 speaker
- 19 special
- 20 spelling
- 21 stretch
- 22 software

- 23 sort criteria
- 24 sort
- 25 order
- 26 sorting
- 27 spelling
- 28 split
- 29 spreadsheet
- 30 square brackets
- 31 stable (software)
- 32 standalone
- 33 standard
- 34 standby
- 35 start page
- 36 start
- 37 startup
- 38 statement
- 39 static IP-address
- 40 statistics
- 41 status
- 42 stop
- 43 storage
- 44 store
- 45 story
- 46 straight quotes

- 47 string (n)
- 48 structure
- 49 stuck
- 50 style sheet
- 51 style
- 52 system

SCROLL LOCK key
    1.   የቁጥር-ቁልፎች-ማስነሻ-ቁልፍ
SHIFT key
    1.   የሺፍት ቁልፍ፤ ቀያሪ ቁልፍ
SQL
    1.   መደበኛ-የመጠይቅ-ቋንቋ
scheme
    1.   መርሃ-ግብር
sequence
    1.   ተከታታይ
    2.   ቅጥልጣይ
sensor
    1.   ሰሚ
serial
    1.   ተከታታይ (parallel=ጎንለጎን)

series

    1.   ተከታታይ

server

    1.   አገልጋይ

    2.   ተጠሪ

    3.   ካዳሚ

    4.   መጋቢ

Service

    1.   ግልጋሎት

Service Pack

    1.   ተጨማሪ-የማሻሻያዎች-ጥቅል

    2.   የመጠገኛ ስብስብ

set

    1.   ሰይም

shading

    1.   ጥላ

sharing

    1.   መጋራት

shell

    1.   ቀፎ

side

    1.   ጎን

spacing

    1.   ክፍተት

speaker

    1.   ተናጋሪ

special

    1.   ልዩ

spelling

    1.   የቃላት አጻጻፍ

stack የስራ-ክምር ste street መንገድ

stretch

    1.   ይዘረጋ

    2.   ዘርጋ

    3.   መዘርጋት

strict ጥብቅ Strikeout ይሰረዝ subtotal ድምር
suggest ምክር suggestion አስተያየት synchronize
ይጣመር save ይኑር ጠብቅ scalable ተመጣኝ scale (v)
ይለካ scale መለኪያ scan (v) ስካን scanner ስካነር
scenario ሁኔታ schedule ቀጠሮ schema ረቂቅ-ንድፍ
screen ስክሪን screensaver ስክሪን-ጠባቂ screenshot
የስክሪን ምስል script መሪ-ጽሑፍ scroll bar
ማንፊቀቂያ-ዘንግ scroll ይንፊቀቅ search engine አሳሽ
ሞተር search ይፈልግ second ሁለተኛ section ክፍል
sectors ክፍሎች secure (n) ደህንነቱ የተጠበቀ secure
(v) ደህንነቱ ይጠበቅ security warning የደህንነት
ማስጠንቀቂያ security ደህንነት see also ይህንንም

ይመለክቲል select all ሁሉም ይመረጥ select ይመረጥ selection ምርጫ selector መራጭ semi-colon የላቲን ነጠላ-ሰረዝ semicolon የላቲን ነጠላ-ሰረዝ send ይላክ sender ላኪ. separator (delimiter) ከፋፋይ server ተጠሪ service አገልግሎት session ክፍለ ጊዜ set as ይሰየም እንደ set to true እውነት ተብሎ ይሰየም set (v) ይሰየም set (n) ስብስብ settings ስየማዎች setup ተከላ shade ጥላ shadow ጥላ share (v) መጋራት share (n) የመጋራት-ደንብ sharpness ስለት sheet ገጣፍ shortcut አቋራጭ show ይታይ shut down ይዘጋ shutdown ይዘጋ sidebar የጎን-ማስጫ sign in ይግቡ sign off ይውጡ signal ምልክት signature ፊርማ simple ቀላል sine ሳይን single-click እንዴ-መጫን site ገጽ size መጠን skip ይዘለል slash መስመር slave (adj) ተከታይ slide ይንሸራተት slider አንሸራታች slow ቀስ-ያለ small capitals በትንሹ የተጻፈ ትልቁ የእንግሊዘኛ ፊደላት small caps በትንሹ የተጻፈ ትልቁ የእንግሊዘኛ ፊደላት smiley የስሜት-ምልክቶች snapshot ምስል
software

1.   ልስልስ እካል

2.   ፕሮግራም

sort criteria

1.   የቅደም-ተከተል ደንብ

sort

1.   በቅደም-ተከተል ይቀመጥ

order

    1.   ቅደም-ተከተል

sorting

    1.   በቅደም-ተከተል በማስቀመጥ ላይ

sound ድምፅ source ምንጭ space ስፍራ spacebar የክፍት-ቦታ ቁልፍ spam (v) ስፓም specify ይገለጽ speech ንግግር speed ፍጥነት spell checker የፊደል-ግድፈት-አራሚ spell checking የፊደል-ግድፈት በማረም ላይ spell-checker የፊደል-ግድፈት-አራሚ

spelling

    1.   ፊደለ.ቀል

split

    1.   ይሰነጠቅ (ግስ)

    2.   ስንጥቅ (ስም)

spreadsheet

    1.   ባለሰንጠረዥ-ማስሊያ

square brackets

    1.   ማዕዘን ቅንፍ

stable (software)

    1.   የተገራ

standalone

    1.   ራሱን-የቻለ

    2.   ራስቻይ

standard

1. መደበኛ

standby

1. ይጠባበቅ (ግስ)
2. ተጠባበቅ (ትዕዕዛዝ)

start page

1. መጀመሪያ ገጽ

start

1. ይጀምር
2. ጀምር

startup

1. ጀማሪ ፕሮግራሞች
2. ቀድሞ ተነሽ ሰልፎች

statement

1. አረፍተ-ነገር

static IP-address

1. ቋሚ የኢንተርኔት ወግ አድራሻ

statistics

1. የቁጥር መረጃ ጥናት
2. ቀመር

status

1. ደረጃ
2. ሁኔታ

stop

    1.   ይቁም

    2.   ቁም

storage

    1.   ካዝና

    2.   ማጎደር

store

    1.   ይኑር

    2.   አኑር

    3.   አስቀምጥ

story

    1.   ታሪክ

straight quotes

    1.   ቀጥታ ጥቅስ

string (n)

    1.   ሐረግ (ስም)

structure

    1.   ቁሚ

    2.   ቅስር

stuck (?)

style sheet

    1.   ዘይቤ ንጣፍ

style

1.   ዘይቤ

subfolder ንዑስ-ደሴ subject line የጉዳይ መስመር
subject ጉዳይ submenu ንዑስ-ምርጫ submit ይግባ
subscribe ይመዝገብ subscription የደምበኝነት-ምዝገባ
subsidiary በስር-የሚስተዳደር substitute ይተካ
substitution መተካት suffix ባዕድ-መድረሻ suite
የተሟላ sum ድምር summary ማጠቃለያ
supplemental ተጨማሪ support ርዳታ surf ይታሰስ
suspend ይቁም switch ይቀየር symbol መለያ-ምልክት
synchronization ማጣመር synonym ተመሳሳይ
syntactical error ሰዋሰው-ስህተት syntax error
የሰዋሰው ስህተት syntax ሰዋሰው

system

1.   ሲስተም

2.   ስርዓት

3.   ገዢ ስልት (OS)

Amharic Computer Glossary – T

- 1 TAB
- 2 tab
- 3 TAB key
- 4 tabular
- 5 TCP (Transmission Control Protocol)
- 6 TCP/IP
- 7 telephone
- 8 tentative
- 9 test
- 10 temporary
- 11 temprature
- 12 terminate
- 13 text editor
- 14 text file
- 15 theme
- 16 thread
- 17 thumbnail
- 18 trap
- 19 trash
- 20 tree
- 21 trend
- 22 trigger

- 23 troubleshoot
- 24 troubleshooting
- 25 true
- 26 truncated
- 27 turn off
- 28 turn on
- 29 two dimensional
- 30 type

TAB

    1.   **አንቀጽ**

tab

    1.   **ገ9ስ መስኮት** (tab browsing)

TAB key

    1.   **የታብ ቁልፍ**

    2.   **የአንቀጽ ቁልፍ**

tabular

    1.   **የሰንጠረዥ**

TCP (Transmission Control Protocol)

    1.   **የሰነድ ማስተላለፊያ መቆጣጠሪያ ወግ**

TCP/IP

    1.   **የሰነድ ማስተላለፍ መቆጣጠሪያና ኢንተርኔት ወግ**

telephone

    1.   ስልክ

tentative

    1.   ጊዜያዊ

test

    1.   ሙከራ

==tight== ጥብቅ tile ድርድር today ዛሬ transform ይለወጥ translate ይተረጎም transparency ውስጠ-ግልፅ try ይሞክር tab key የታብ ቁልፍ tab የታብ መጥሪያ table of contents የማውጫ ሡንጠረዥ table ሡንጠረዥ tag ማስታወሻ tangent ታንጀንት tape ቴፕ target ግብ task ተግባር taskbar የተግባር ማስጫ template ንድፍ

temporary

    1.   ጊዚያዊ

temperature

    1.   ሙቀዜ (ሙቀት/ቅዝቃዜ)

terminate

    1.   ይቋጭ

text editor

    1.   ጽሑፍ አራሚ

text file

    1.   የጽሑፍ ሰነድ

    2.   የጽሑፍ ፋይል

    text ጽሑፍ textbox የጽሑፍ ሰጥን texture ገፀታ

theme

    1.   ጭብጥ

    2.   ገጽታ

thread

    1.   ሐረግ

thumbnail

    1.   ናሙና

tilde ጭረት time elapsed ያለፈ ጊዜ time remaining ቀሪ ጊዜ time stamp የሰዓት ማኅተም time ጊዜ timeout ጊዜ-አለፈበት tip ምክር tips ምክሮች title አርዕስት toggle ይቀየር token ጥቅል tool መሣሪያ ==toolbar== የመሣሪያ ማስጭ ==toolbox== የመሣሪያ ሳጥን, የስራ ሳጥን top ላይ topic አርዕስት total row ጠቅላላ ረድፍ total ጠቅላላ track ክትትል ይደረግበት trademark የንግድ ምልክት transaction ልውውጥ transfer (v) ይተላለፍ transfer (n) ማስተላለፍ transition ሽግግር transmission ማስተላለፍ transmit ይተላለፍ transparent ውስጠ-ግልፅ

trap

    1.   ወጥመድ

trash

    1.   ትቢያ

    2.   የማያስፈልግ

tree

    1.   ዛፍ፡

trend

    1.   የጊዜው-ወግ

trigger

    1.   ይንቀሳቀስ

troubleshoot

    1.   ለችግር-መፍትሄ-ይፈልግ

troubleshooting

    1.   ለችግር-መፍትሄ-በመፈለግ-ላይ

true

    1.   እውነት

truncated

    1.   የተጣጠፈ

turn off

    1.   ይጥፉ

turn on

    1.   ይብራ

two dimensional

    1.   ሁለት ልክ

    2.   ባለሁለት አቅጣጫ

type

    1.   ዓይነት

Amharic Computer Glossary – U

- 1 URL (Uniform Resource Locator)
- 2 Unicode
- 3 User name
- 4 unavailable
- 5 uncheck (a check box)
- 6 undelete
- 7 underline
- 8 underscore
- 9 undo
- 10 uninstall
- 11 unique
- 12 unit
- 13 unmount
- 14 unread
- 15 unsubscribe
- 16 untitled
- 17 update
- 18 upgrade (v)
- 19 upload
- 20 uppercase

URL (Uniform Resource Locator)

    1.   የሰነድ አድራሻ

Unicode

    1.   ዩኒኮድ

User name

    1.   የተጠቃሚ ስም

unavailable

    1.   አልተገኘም

uncheck (a check box)

    1.   አይረገጥ

undelete

    1.   አይሰረዝ

underline

    1.   ከስር-መስመር ይሰመር

underscore

    1.   የስር-መስመር

undo

    1.   አይደረግ

uninstall

    1.   ይነቀል

unique

    1.   ልዩ

unit

    1.   አሃድ

    2.   መስፈርት

unmount

    1.   አይጫን

    2.   አውርድ

    3.   አውጣ

unread

    1.   አይነበብ

unsubscribe

    1.   ምዝገባው-ይሰረዝ

untitled

    1.   ያልተሰየመ

update

    1.   ይሻሻል

    2.   አሻሽል

upgrade (v)

    1.   ይሻሻል

    2.   ይሻሻል

upload

    1.   ይላክ

    2.   ላክ

    3.   ይሰደድ

4. ስደድ

5. ጨን

6. ይጨን

uppercase

1. የእንግሊዘኛ ትልቅ ፊደል

==use (v)== ይጠቀሟል ==user== ተጠቃሚ
==username== የተጠቃሚ-ስም ==utilities==
መገልገያዎች

Amharic Computer Glossary – V

- 1 valid
- 2 variable
- 3 verify
- 4 version
- 5 view (v)
- 6 view (n)
- 7 virtual
- 8 visible
- 9 visibility
- 10 virus
- 11 volume

valid

    1.   **ተቀባይነት-ያለው**

variable

    1.   **ተለዋጭ**

verify

    1.   **አረጋገጥ**

    2.   **ይረጋገጥ**

version

    1.   **ዝርያ**

view (v)

    1.   ይመለከቲል

view (n)

    1.   እይታ (ስ)

virtual

    1.   መሳይ

    2.   መሰል

visible

    1.   ታዪ

    2.   የሚታይ

visibility

    1.   ታዪነት

virus

    1.   ቫይረስ

volume

    1.   መጠን

    2.   ይዘት

Amharic Computer Glossary – W

- 1 WWW (World Wide Web)
- 2 wait
- 3 tutorial
- 4 weekday
- 5 weekly
- 6 weight
- 7 wrap
- 8 wallpaper
- 9 wireless
- 10 wireless access point

WWW (World Wide Web)

1. መመመ (መረጃ መቀባበያ መረብ)

wait

1. ጠብቅ
2. ቆይ

tutorial

1. መለማመጃ
2. መልመጃ

weekday

1. አዘቦት ቀን

weekly

   1.   ሳምንታዊ

weight

   1.   ክብደት

wrap

   1.   መጠቅለል

wallpaper

   1.   የጓላ-ምስል

warn (v) ያስጠነቅቁል warning message ማስጠንቀቂያ መልዕክት warning ማስጠንቀቂያ watch ይመለከቷል web page የመረብ ገጽ web መረብ webmaster ሊቀ-መረብ website የመረብ-ገጽ widget እጀታ width ስፋት wildcard ጃከር window መስኮት

wireless

   1.   ሽቦ አልባ

wireless access point

   1.   ሽቦ አልባ መግቢያ ጣቢያ

wizard አስማተኛ word processor ቃላት-ቀማሪ word ቃል workgroup የስራ-ቡድን worksheet የስራ-ንጣፍ workspace የስራ-ገበታ workstation ኮምፒተር wrap ይሸፈን write ይጻፍ write-protected ከመጻፍ-የተገደበ

Amharic Computer Glossary – X

xerox

    1.   xerox

x-ray

    1.   **ኤክስ ጨረር**

x-windows

    1.   x-windows

Amharic Computer Glossary – Y

year

    1.   ዓመት

yes

    1.   አዎ

Amharic Computer Glossary – Z

- 1 ZIP code
- 2 zone
- 3 zoom
- 4 zoomin
- 5 zoomout

ZIP code
    1.   **የዚፕ ኮድ**

zone
    1.   **ዞን**

zoom
    1.   **አዙም**
    2.   **መጣኝ**

zoomin
    1.   **መጠን አሳዳጊ**

zoomout
    1.   **መጠን አሳናሽ**

APPENDIX A & B

As Compiled & edited by the
LOJ Society Tech. Dept.,
LOJ-encyclopedia

Bit (ቢ.ት)

v • d • e Multiples of bits				
SI prefixes			**Binary prefixes**	
Name (Symbol)	Standard SI	Binary usage	Name (Symbol)	Value
kilobit (kbit)	10^3	2^{10}	kibibit (Kibit)	2^{10}
megabit (Mbit)	10^6	2^{20}	mebibit (Mibit)	2^{20}
gigabit (Gbit)	10^9	2^{30}	gibibit (Gibit)	2^{30}
terabit (Tbit)	10^{12}	2^{40}	tebibit (Tibit)	2^{40}
petabit (Pbit)	10^{15}	2^{50}	pebibit (Pibit)	2^{50}
exabit (Ebit)	10^{18}	2^{60}	exbibit (Eibit)	2^{60}
zettabit (Zbit)	10^{21}	2^{70}	zebibit (Zibit)	2^{70}
yottabit (Ybit)	10^{24}	2^{80}	yobibit (Yobit)	2^{80}

(Yibit)

These articles are about bits, bytes and related the unit(s) of information.

A bit is a <u>binary</u> <u>digit</u>, taking a value of either 0 or 1. Binary digits are a basic unit of <u>information storage</u> and <u>communication</u> in digital <u>computing</u> and digital <u>information theory</u>. Information theory also often uses the natural digit, called either a *<u>nit</u>* or a *<u>nat</u>*. <u>Quantum computing</u> also uses <u>qubits</u>, a single piece of information with a probability of being true.

The bit is also a unit of measurement, the information capacity of one binary digit. It has the symbol bit, or b (see discussion below).

Appendix A – Contents

- 1 Binary digit

- 2 Representation
o 2.1 Transmission
o 2.2 Storage

- 3 Unit

- 4 Abbreviation and symbol

- 5 Multiple bits

- 6 See also

- 7 Notes

Binary digit

<u>Claude E. Shannon</u> first used the word *bit* in his 1948 paper *A Mathematical Theory of Communication*. He attributed its origin to <u>John W. Tukey</u>, who had written a Bell Labs memo on 9 January 1947 in which he contracted "binary digit" to simply "bit". Interestingly, <u>Vannevar Bush</u> had written in 1936 of "bits of information" that could be stored on the <u>punch cards</u> used in the mechanical computers of that time. [1]

A bit of storage can be either on (1) or off (0). A single bit is a one or a zero, a true or a false, a "flag" which is "on" or "off", or in general, the quantity of information required to distinguish two mutually exclusive equally probable *states* from each other. <u>Gregory Bateson</u> defined a bit as "a difference which makes a difference".[2]

Representation

Transmission

Bits can be implemented in many forms depending on context. For example, in <u>digital circuitry</u> in most computing devices as well as flash memories, a bit is an <u>electrical</u> pulse generated by the internal clock in the control unit or data register. For devices using <u>positive logic</u>, a logical 1 (true value) is represented by up to 5 <u>volts</u>, while a logical 0 (false value) is represented by 0 volt.

Storage

Bits are manipulated in the <u>volatile memory</u> of a computer, and can further be kept in a persistent manner on a <u>magnetic storage</u> device such as magnetic tape or disc, as well as on <u>optical discs</u>.

Unit

It is important to differentiate between the use of "bit" in referring to a discrete storage unit and the use of "bit" in referring to a statistical unit of information. The bit, as a discrete storage unit, can by definition store only 0 or 1. A statistical bit is the amount of information that, *on average*, can be stored in a discrete bit. It is thus the amount of information carried by a choice between two equally likely outcomes. One bit corresponds to about 0.693 <u>nats</u> ($\ln(2)$), or 0.301 <u>hartleys</u> ($\log_{10}(2)$).

Consider, for example, a <u>computer file</u> with one thousand 0s and 1s which can be <u>losslessly compressed</u> to a file of five hundred 0s and 1s (on average, over all files of that kind). The original file, although having 1,000 bits of storage, has at most 500 bits of <u>information entropy</u>, since information is not destroyed by lossless compression. A file can have no more information theoretical bits than it has storage bits. If these two ideas need to be distinguished, sometimes the name *bit* is used when discussing data storage while *shannon* is used for the statistical bit. However, most of the time, the meaning is clear from the context.

Abbreviation and symbol

No uniform agreements exist, neither amongst the standards bodies, nor the affected technical disciplines, regarding an official designation of a symbol for the units *bit* and *byte*. One commonly-quoted standard, the International Electrotechnical Commission's IEC 60027, specifies that the bit should have the symbol *bit*, used in all multiples, such as "kbit" (for kilobit). In the same documents, the symbols "o" and "B" are specified for the byte.

Today the harmonized ISO/IEC IEC 80000-13:2008 standard cancels and replaces subclauses 3.8 and 3.9 of IEC 60027-2:2005 (those related to information theory and prefixes for binary multiples).

The other commonly-quoted relevant standard, IEEE 1541, specifies "b" to be the unit symbol for bit and "B" to be that for byte. This convention is also widely used in computing, but has so far not been considered acceptable internationally for several reasons:

- both these symbols are already used for other units: "b" for barn and "B" for bel. The unit *bel* is rarely used by itself, but usually as decibel (dB), which is unlikely to be confused with a decibyte. The chances of conflict with "B" for byte are small, even though both units are very commonly used in the same fields (e.g., telecommunication).

- *bit* is already a contraction of "binary digit", so there is little reason to abbreviate it further;

- it is customary to start a unit symbol with an uppercase letter only if the unit was named after a person (see also Claude Émile Jean-Baptiste Litre);

- instead of byte, the term octet (unit symbol: "o") is used in some fields and in some Francophone countries, which adds to the difficulty of agreeing on an international symbol;

- "b" is occasionally also used for byte, along with "bit" for bit.

Multiple bits

A byte is a collection of bits, which may differ in size but the standard at present is almost always eight bits. Eight-bit bytes, also known as *octets*, can represent 256 values (2^8 values, 0–255). A four-bit quantity is known as a *nibble*, and can represent 16 values (2^4 values, 0–15). A rarely used term, *crumb*, can refer to a two-bit quantity, and can represent 4 values (2^2 values, 0–3).

"Word" is a term for a slightly larger group of bits, but it has no standard size. It represents the size of one register in a Computer-CPU. In the IA-32 architecture more commonly known as x86-32, 16 bits are called a "word" (with 32 bits being a double word or dword), but other architectures have word sizes of 8, 32, 64, 80 or others.

Terms for large quantities of bits can be formed using the standard range of SI prefixes, e.g., kilobit (kbit), megabit (Mbit) and gigabit (Gbit). Note that much confusion exists regarding these units and their abbreviations, due in part to the issues above and in part to the issues surrounding binary prefixes.

When a bit within a group of bits such as a byte or word is to be referred to, it is usually specified by a number from 0 (not 1) upwards corresponding to its position within the byte or word. However, 0 can refer to either the most significant bit or to the least significant bit depending on the context, so the convention being used must be known.

Certain bitwise computer processor instructions (such as *bit set*) operate at the level of manipulating bits rather than manipulating data interpreted as an aggregate of bits.

Telecommunications or computer network transfer rates are usually described in terms of bits per second (*bit/s*), not to be confused with baud.

See also

- Units of information
- Byte
- Integral data type
- Bitstream
- Information entropy
- Binary arithmetic
- Ternary numeral system

Notes

1. ^ *Darwin among the machines: the evolution of global intelligence*, George Dyson, 1997. ISBN 0-201-40649-7

2. ^ Social Systems

Byte ባይት(ቶች)

Compiled & edited by LOJ Society Tech. Dept.,
LOJ-encyclopedia

Prefixes for <u>bit</u> and byte multiples				
Decimal		Binary		
Value	SI	Value	IEC	JEDEC
1000 k <u>kilo-</u>		1024 Ki <u>kibi-</u>		K <u>kilo-</u>
1000^2 M <u>mega-</u>		1024^2 Mi <u>mebi-</u>		M <u>mega-</u>
1000^3 G <u>giga-</u>		1024^3 Gi <u>gibi-</u>		G <u>giga-</u>
1000^4 T <u>tera-</u>		1024^4 Ti <u>tebi-</u>		
1000^5 P <u>peta-</u>		1024^5 Pi <u>pebi-</u>		
1000^6 E <u>exa-</u>		1024^6 Ei <u>exbi-</u>		
1000^7 Z <u>zetta-</u>		1024^7 Zi <u>zebi-</u>		
1000^8 Y <u>yotta-</u>		1024^8 Yi <u>yobi-</u>		

A byte (pronounced IPA: / baɪ t/) is a basic unit of measurement of <u>information storage</u> in <u>computer science</u>. In many <u>computer architectures</u> it is a <u>unit of</u> memory <u>addressing</u>.

There is no standard but a byte most often consists of eight bits.

A byte is an ordered collection of bits, with each bit denoting a single binary value of 1 or 0. The byte most often consists of 8 bits in modern systems, however, the size of a byte can vary and is generally determined by the underlying computer operating system or hardware. Historically, byte size was determined by the number of bits required to represent a single character from a Western character set. Its size was generally determined by the number of possible characters in the supported character set and was chosen to be a divisor of the computer's word size. Historically bytes have ranged from five to twelve bits.

The popularity of IBM's System/360 architecture starting in the 1960s and the explosion of microcomputers based on 8-bit microprocessors in the 1980s has made eight bits by far the most common size for a byte. The term octet is widely used as a more precise synonym where ambiguity is undesirable (for example, in protocol definitions).

There has been considerable confusion about the meanings of metric -- or SI prefixes -- used with the word "byte", especially concerning prefixes such as kilo- (k or K) and mega- (M) as shown in the chart *Prefixes for bit and byte*. Since computer memory is designed with dual logic, multiples are expressed in <u>power of two</u>, rather than 10, the software and computer industries often use binary estimates of the SI-prefixed quantities, while producers of computer storage devices prefer the SI values. This is the reason for specifying computer hard drive capacities of, say, "100 GB" when it contains 93 GiB (or 93 GB in traditional units) of addressable storage. Because of the confusion, a contract specifying a quantity of bytes must define what the prefixes mean in terms of the contract (i.e., the alternative binary equivalents or the actual decimal values, or a binary estimate based on the actual values).

To make the meaning of the table absolutely clear: A <u>kibibyte</u> (KiB) is 1,024 bytes. A <u>mebibyte</u> (MiB) is 1,024 × 1,024 or 1,048,576 bytes. The figures in the column using 1,024 raised to powers of 1, 2, 3, 4 and so on are in units of bytes.

Appendix B – Contents

- 1 Meanings

- 2 History

- 3 Alternative words

- 4 Abbreviation/Symbol

- 5 See also

- 6 Notes

Meanings

The word "byte" ባይት(ቶች) has two closely related meanings:

1. A contiguous sequence of a *fixed* number of <u>bits</u> (binary digits). The use of a byte to mean 8 bits has become nearly ubiquitous.

2. A contiguous sequence of bits within a binary computer that comprises the *smallest addressable sub-field* of the computer's natural <u>word</u>-size. That is, the smallest unit of binary data on which meaningful computation, or natural data boundaries, could be applied. For example, the <u>CDC 6000 series</u> scientific mainframes divided their 60-bit floating-point words into 10 six-bit bytes. These bytes conveniently held <u>Hollerith</u> data from punched cards, typically the upper-case alphabet and decimal digits. CDC also often referred to 12-bit quantities as bytes, each holding two 6-bit <u>display code</u> characters, due to the 12-bit I/O architecture of the machine. The <u>PDP-10</u> used assembly instructions LDB and DPB to extract bytes — these operations survive today in <u>Common Lisp</u>. Bytes of six, seven, or nine bits were used on some computers, for example within the 36-bit word of the <u>PDP-10</u>. The <u>UNIVAC</u>

1100/2200 series computers (now Unisys) addressed in both 6-bit (Fieldata) and 9-bit (ASCII) modes within its 36-bit word.

History

The term byte was coined by Dr. Werner Buchholz in July 1956, during the early design phase for the IBM Stretch computer.[123] Originally it was defined in instructions by a 4-bit byte-size field, allowing from one to sixteen bits (the production design reduced this to a 3-bit byte-size field, allowing from one to eight bits to be represented by a byte); typical I/O equipment of the period used six-bit bytes. A fixed eight-bit byte size was later adopted and promulgated as a standard by the System/360. The term "byte" comes from "bite," as in the smallest amount of data a computer could "bite" at once. The spelling change not only reduced the chance of a "bite" being mistaken for a "bit," but also was consistent with the penchant of early computer scientists to make up words and change spellings. A byte was also often referred to as "an 8-bit byte", reinforcing the notion that it was a tuple of n bits, and that other sizes were possible.

1. A contiguous sequence of binary bits in a serial data stream, such as in modem or satellite communications, or from a disk-

drive head, which is the smallest meaningful unit of data. These bytes might include start bits, stop bits, or parity bits, and thus could vary from 7 to 12 bits to contain a single 7-bit ASCII code.

2. A *datatype* or synonym for a datatype in certain underlying programming languages. C and C++, for example, defines *byte* as "addressable unit of data large enough to hold any member of the basic character set of the execution environment" (clause 3.6 of the C standard). Since the C char integral data type must contain at least 8 bits (clause 5.2.4.2.1), a byte in C is at least capable of holding 256 different values (signed or unsigned char does not matter). Various implementations of C and C++ define a "byte" as 8, 9, 16, 32, or 36 bits[45]. The actual number of bits in a particular implementation is documented as CHAR_BIT as implemented in the limits.h file. Java's primitive byte data type is always defined as consisting of 8 bits and being a signed data type, holding values from −128 to 127.

Early microprocessors, such as Intel 8008 (the direct predecessor of the 8080, and then 8086) could perform a small number of operations on four bits, such as the DAA (decimal adjust) instruction, and the "half carry" flag, that were used to implement decimal arithmetic routines. These four-bit quantities were called "nybbles," in homage to the then-common 8-bit "bytes."

Alternative words

Following "bit," "byte," and "nybble," there have been some analogical attempts to construct unambiguous terms for bit blocks of other sizes.[6] All of these are strictly jargon, and not very common.

- 2 bits: crumb, quad, quarter, tayste, tydbit

- 4 bits: nibble, nybble

- 5 bits: nickel, nyckle

- 10 bits: deckle

- 13 bits: baker's byte

- 16 bits: plate, playte, chomp, chawmp (on a 32-bit machine)

- 18 bits: chomp, chawmp (on a 36-bit machine)

- 32 bits: dinner, dynner, gawble (on a 286 ryan m-bit machine)

- 48 bits: gobble, gawble (under circumstances that remain obscure)

Abbreviation/Symbol

<u>IEEE 1541</u> and <u>Metric-Interchange-Format</u> specify "B" as the symbol for byte (e.g. MB means megabyte), while <u>IEC 60027</u> seems silent on the subject. Furthermore, B means bel (see <u>decibel</u>), another (logarithmic) unit used in the same field. The use of B to stand for bel is consistent with the metric system convention that capitalized symbols are for units named after a person (in this case <u>Alexander Graham Bell</u>); usage of a capital B to stand for byte is not consistent with this convention. There is little danger of confusing a byte with a bel because the bel's sub-multiple the <u>decibel</u> (dB) is usually preferred, while use of the decibyte (dB) is extremely rare.

The unit symbol "kb" with a lowercase "b" is a commonly used abbreviation for "kilobyte". Use of this abbreviation leads to confusion with the alternative use of "kb" to mean "<u>kilobit</u>". IEEE 1541 specifies "b" as the symbol for <u>bit</u>; however the <u>IEC</u> 60027 and Metric-Interchange-Format specify "bit" (e.g. Mbit for megabit) for the symbol, achieving maximum disambiguation from byte.

French-speaking countries sometimes use an uppercase "o" for "octet". This is not consistent with <u>SI</u> because of the risk of confusion with the zero, and the convention that capitals are reserved for unit names derived from proper names, such as the ampere (whose symbol is A) and joule (symbol J), versus the second (symbol s) and metre (symbol m).

Lowercase "o" for "octet" is a commonly used symbol in several non-English-speaking countries, and is also used with metric prefixes (for example, "ko" and "Mo").

Today the harmonized ISO/IEC IEC 80000-13:2008 - Quantities and units -- Part 13: Information science and technology standard cancels and replaces subclauses 3.8 and 3.9 of IEC 60027-2:2005 (those related to Information theory and Prefixes for binary multiples). See Units of information#Byte for detailed discussion on names for derived units.

See also

- Bit

- Word (computing)

Notes

1. ^ Origins of the Term "BYTE" Bob Bemer, accessed 2007-08-12

2. ^ TIMELINE OF THE IBM STRETCH/HARVEST ERA (1956–1961) computerhistory.org, '1956 July ... Werner

Buchholz ... Werner's term "Byte" first popularized'

3. ^ byte catb.org, 'coined by Werner Buchholz in 1956'

4. ^ 26 Built-in / intrinsic / primitive data types, C++ FAQ Lite

5. ^ Integer Types In C and C

6. ^ nybble reference.com sourced from Jargon File 4.2.0, accessed 2007-08-12